THE
SEVENTH SEAL

BY A STUDENT OF
THE ORDER OF CHRISTIAN MYSTICS

THE SEVENTH SEAL

Teachings of The Order of Christian Mystics
The "Curtiss Books" freely available at
www.orderofchristianmystics.co.za

1. The Voice of Isis
2. The Message of Aquaria
3. The Inner Radiance
4. Realms of the Living Dead
5. Coming World Changes
6. The Key to the Universe
7. The Key of Destiny
8. Letters from the Teacher Volume I
9. Letters from the Teacher Volume II
10. The Truth about Evolution and the Bible
11. The Philosophy of War
12. Personal Survival
13. The Pattern Life
14. Four-Fold Health
15. Vitamins
16. Why Are We Here?
17. Reincarnation
18. For Young Souls
19. Gems of Mysticism
20. The Temple of Silence
21. The Divine Mother
22. The Soundless Sound
23. The Mystic Life
24. The Love of Rabiacca
25. Potent Prayers

Supporting Volumes

26. The Seventh Seal
27. Towards the Light

THE
SEVENTH SEAL

BY
JEANETTE AGNES

*And when he had opened the seventh
seal, there was silence in heaven about
the space of half an hour.*
Revelation 8: i.

2014 EDITION

REPUBLISHED FOR THE ORDER BY
MOUNT LINDEN PUBLISHING
JOHANNESBURG, SOUTH AFRICA
ISBN: 978-1-920483-07-4

"Ministers of Christ and Stewards of the Mysteries of God."
1 Corinthians 4 vs. 1

COPYRIGHT 2014

BY
MOUNT LINDEN PUBLISHING

First Published in 1920

May be used for non-commercial, personal, research and educational use.
ALL RIGHTS RESERVED

DEDICATED

TO ALL MEN EVERYWHERE

———

Have we not all one Father?
Hath not one God created us?
Malachi 2: 10.

PREFACE

I deplore any suggestion of cowardice which may attach to my incomplete signature, but for reasons which I may not state, it is fitting that this be published under my given names only.

JEANETTE AGNES.

TABLE OF CONTENTS

CHAPTER		PAGE
	Introduction	9
I	What Shall We Say of Matter?	13
II	The Lost Word	20
III	"Things Which Have Been Kept Secret From the Foundation of the World." Matt. 13:35	25
IV	Search the Scriptures	37
V	The Fire of the Lord	74
VI	A Glance at Fundamentals	122
VII	The Way of Attainment	140

INTRODUCTION

The object of this brief treatise is to explain the spiritual significance of the Levitical Law in connection with the Holy of Holies of the Tabernacle, and its relation to the truth that souls are created with distinct male and female capacities and powers: to show that the soul may be at rest and the individual ready for the development of powers which transcend what are termed human possibilities when the man and woman possessing the dual expressions of the same soul have been united in the one perfect love relation: That it is possible when spiritual discernment has been sufficiently developed, to know without error the complement of one's own soul: that the Bible teaches that the law of the creative life energy, operating through the physical sex of soul complements, is, through the power of its spiritual reality, the way of the refinement and spiritualization of the matter of which our bodies are composed—the way of emancipation from want, sickness, and all imperfections of the human race; in truth, the way of eternal life without the body's passing through what we call death: that concerning this is the mystery—the hidden power in the meaning of the Holy Name—the Lost Word which has been sought through the ages: that both prevailing beliefs in regard to matter must be altered before we can be liberated from the bondage of materiality; and briefly to indicate the kind of spiritual development necessary thus to attain to the Kingdom.

The statements made herein as truth, it is needless to say, are my convictions of truth, founded upon experience, thought, study, or the testimony within me of the Spirit of Truth Itself, which Jesus promised should be given to lead us into all truth.

I readily grant that the claims made are extraordinary, and I have reason to believe there may be noble souls who, upon first impression, will think my message not a worthy one; but being convinced beyond all doubt that these are the significant facts underlying Biblical symbol and allegory, and realizing the inestimable value in every way to the human family of a right understanding of God's plan for happiness, and the continuity of life, and the reason why these never can be found until men seek the Lord with the whole heart, you may appreciate something of the urge which has impelled me to speak; indeed, which will grant me no rest until I have spoken, even at the risk of any and all kinds of criticism in regard to my sanity, my motives and my personal character; and I would ask of every reader, if these be not worthy objects which I thus wish to further, what then shall we say constitutes worth?

Nor can I heed the admonitions, though all so kindly meant, of any who would stay me from my task, even though I should incur the disrespect of those from whom respect would be most valued, for the dreariest outlook can in no wise excuse one for shirking what he clearly sees to be his duty and opportunity for service.

Know then, my friends, when in "The Way of Attainment" I urge you always to follow the highest light you have—know then where it may lead you; know what determination to do the right under any and all circumstances it may demand of you. But *follow* it, alone if need be, "O'er moor and fen, o'er *crag and torrent*, till the night is gone." There *is* no other way.

CHAPTER I

WHAT SHALL WE SAY OF MATTER?

AS the truth set forth in the following pages is concerned with the fact that not only is matter real, but that contrary to accepted belief, it is a part of God Himself, I wish to direct attention briefly to this subject at the outset.

Both of the current beliefs, on the one hand that matter is nothing; on the other hand, that it is a thing apart from God, lead to confusion and errors in living, because of the fact that they give rise to the belief that some part of our being may exist apart from a spiritual reality.

We hear it commonly said that God animates matter, that God is *in* matter, but this presupposes that God and matter are two wholly different things. I say matter is a part of God—God's body, so to speak, for if matter is no part of God, then God is not all; hence not God. It is evident that matter is essential as a medium through which God may manifest his life. If matter did not exist, there could be no expression of God's life; but if God needs matter through which to manifest' his life, and must go outside of Himself to have it supplied from some other source, then God is not complete; He must acknowledge obligations to another power; therefore He would not be God. That would be as if God had the executive ability to organize and conduct a business, but did not have the necessary capital to invest, and must seek a partner. I speak neither facetiously nor irreverently. The cases are parallel.

Because all forms of matter are reducible to one universal substance, and into such form as to be invisible to the physical eye, does not mean that matter can be destroyed, as some are so ready to state, and that in the name of science. When we place a piece of ice in a pan, and apply sufficient heat to turn it first to water and eventually to vapor which will float over our heads, we have not destroyed the matter of which the ice was composed, although we have transformed this substance from a state of density in which it was heavier than air, and by the law of gravitation would fall to the floor if released from the hand, to a rarified state in which it was lighter than air and would rise instead of fall.

No physicist would think of saying that when a piece of iron has been reduced to the gaseous state, the material of which the metal was composed before the law of molecular attraction was overcome by heat, has been destroyed; and it is no more reasonable for him to say that matter can be destroyed because it can be transformed into a state of rarity and vibratory activity beyond the domain of physical science alone to detect and study.

If perchance the ultra-idealist, who will tell you that matter is not real, but merely a mode of thinking, has in mind the wonderful facts of the transformation of matter, he should make this clear, for even reducing it to a point of strain between the negative and positive particles of electricity does not make it unreal. If we contend that a thing is unreal merely because we cannot see it in all its manifestations, we may as well say Spirit is unreal. No one will dispute the fact that organized *forms* of matter are not *permanent*, but when we speak of matter, we rightly mean the atom or electron, or the infinitesimal divisions into which this may yet be said to be divided.

All this apparently unintelligent substance serves us, and is a certain manifestation of God. Our clothes, our food, our houses, the air we breathe and the earth under our feet is God, as well as our mind and Spirit, and our emotions of love and joy. And thus it becomes literally true that "in Him we live and move and have our being." It is not sufficient to say that God is *in* matter. It is either a question of God *and* matter, co-existent, eternal, or God *as* matter. If it is a case of God *and* matter, God is not all. There is no evading this fact for anyone who is willing to give the truth right of way against preconceived ideas. Of course to those who have nestled in some form of belief from which they would not be disturbed at any cost, and hence are not willing to meet the issue squarely with themselves, there is as yet no means of appeal, but time and experience, though it should require another incarnation to accomplish it, will result in the necessary mental honesty.

I grant this view of matter is one for which we have not the customary proof or conclusive form of statement, yet which we know by this process of reasoning must be true; as for instance, the value of the decimal statement of the quotient of 10 divided by 3. By any rule of mathematics with which we are now familiar, the quotient will be 3.3333 on into infinity. We cannot arrive at an exact statement of the value in this form. Nevertheless we know by a certain course of reasoning that the value is $\frac{1}{3}$. And so I say there are some things which, from the very nature of the case, we know to be true, although we may not be able to demonstrate the fact according to customary methods. Even yet the existence of ether is not a *demonstrated* fact. I say this on the authority of one of the prominent scientists of our country. He told me they simply *assume* that such a medium exists, because an intelligent and satisfactory explanation of the phenomena of nature *requires that such a medium should exist*. This, then, is a perfectly logical conclusion to which no one need object, and while it is *obliged* to acknowledge kinship to the processes of faith and intuition (however disconcerting this may be to the materialistic scientist), it also satisfies our reason.

The foregoing arithmetical analogy was employed by the scientist of whom I speak, in this same conversation, but it applies with as much force to the belief that matter is one manifestation of the Absolute as it does to the belief in the existence of ether, which scientists find themselves obliged to accept though not demonstrated by so-called scientific methods. Therefore, I say in words the most untaught may understand, and the erudite cannot gainsay—Matter is a part of God because there is nothing else for it to be if God is *all*. The following excerpt from a lecture on "The Ether and Its Functions", by Sir Oliver Lodge, makes it easier, I think, to formulate a conception of how this might be true, and brings us to the threshold of the full realization:

"I have endeavored to introduce to you the simplest conception of the material universe which has yet occurred to man—that is of one universal substance perfectly homogeneous and continuous and simple of structure, extending to the farthest limits of space of which we have any knowledge, existing equally everywhere, some portions either at rest or in simple, irrational motion, transmitting the undulations which we call light; other portions in rotational motion—in vortices, that is, and differentiated permanently from the rest of the medium by reason of this motion. These whirling portions constitute what we call matter; their motion gives them rigidity, and of them our bodies and all other bodies are built up—one continuous substance filling all space, which can vibrate as light, which can be sheared off into positive and negative electricity, which in whirls constitutes matter, and which transmits by continuity and not by impact every action and reaction of which matter is capable."

We believe that God is all, but we cannot harmonize this belief with evident fact, and still ignore the existence of matter—the very thing we find necessary for the expression of the life of God—but rather by including it with the power and usefulness belonging to it, in God. And since this is true, it should be lifted up and spiritualized, as we shall see more clearly from the succeeding chapters.

CHAPTER II

THE LOST WORD

IN explaining the hidden meaning of the Holy Name, I shall quote at some length from "Bible Mystery and Bible Meaning", by the late Judge T. Troward, for to him we are indebted for the clue to the secret power of the Lost Word. To me it was given to know the interpretation of the mystery of the Holy of Holies of the Tabernacle, but I should not have known that this coincided with the secret power of the Holy Name except for the author's accurate work in interpreting the meaning of the Hebrew letters composing the word "YEVE" (JEHOVAH).

"A point that can hardly fail to strike the Bible student is the frequency with which we are directed to the *Name* of the Lord, as the source of strength and protection, instead of to God Himself, and the steady uniformity of this practice, both in the Old and New Testaments, clearly indicates the intention to put us upon some special line of inquiry with regard to the Sacred Name. Not only is this suggested by the frequency of the expression, but the Bible gives a very remarkable instance which shows that the Sacred Name must be considered as a formula containing a summary of all Wisdom.

"The Master tells us that the Queen of the South came to hear the wisdom of Solomon, and if we turn to I Kings X:1, we find that the fame of Solomon's wisdom, which induced the Queen of Sheba to come to prove him with hard questions was 'concerning the *Name* of the Lord!" This accords with the immemorial tradition of the Jews that the knowledge of the secret name of God enables him who possesses it to perform the most stupendous miracles. This Hidden Name—the 'Schem-hammaphoraseh'—was revealed, they say, to Moses and taught by him to Aaron and handed on by him to his successor; it was the secret enshrined in the Holy of Holies, and was scrupulously guarded by the successive High Priests; it is the supreme secret, and its knowledge is the supreme object of attainment; thus tradition and Scripture alike point to 'The NAME' as the source of Light and Life, and deliverance from all evil.

"May we not therefore suppose that this must be the veiled statement of some great Truth? The purpose of a name is to call up, by a single word, the complete idea of the thing named, with all those qualities and relations that make it what it is, instead of having to describe all this in detail every time we want to suggest the conception of it. The correct name of a thing thus conveys the idea of its whole nature, and accordingly the correct Name of God should, in some manner, be a concise statement of the Divine Nature as the Source of all Life, Wisdom, Power and Goodness and the Origin of all manifested being."

To summarize the explanation which the author gives of the Hebrew Name of God, "YEVE", which in English is "JEHOVAH", he shows by successive, careful steps the meaning of each part of the word. This is found to be *Essential Life* and *Derived Life*, standing in the relation of *masculine* to *feminine*, Y indicating Essential Life, while the second part of the Name—EVE—indicates Derived Feminine Life. Now we see the expression of this masculine and feminine life to be *combined* in *one* name, therefore we are wholly within the truth when speaking of the one *named* as TWO IN ONE.

The author also gives a further explanation of the word by which God's triune nature is seen to be expressed, but we have long been familiar with the thought of the Trinity. We think of God as ONE and as THREE IN ONE, but we have not yet realized the fact that God is also TWO IN ONE, and herein lies "the mystery of God". TWO IN ONE may then be said to be the physical form of the Holy Name which expresses its general nature and power, and which may be passed from lip to lip; but its vital power—its spiritual reality—or let us say, its soul, as far transcends its physical expression as our Spirits transcend in glory our physical bodies, and may not thus be freely spoken of, but must be realized by each one as he is guided into this truth by the Spirit.

With this light on the derivation of the Holy Name, which, as we shall see later, shows it to corroborate the revelation of the meaning of the imagery of the Tabernacle, and the ordinances concerning it, ascribed to

Moses, we now get the full force of Exodus 34:5. "And the Lord descended in the cloud and stood with him there, and *proclaimed the Name of the Lord.*"

But even with this analysis of the meaning of the letters composing the Sacred Name, it remains simply a formula, and we continually overlook its practical application, and the availability of its power to really accomplish the miraculous results for humankind without the correct solution of the symbology of the Tabernacle. This power is said to be "the secret enshrined in the Holy of Holies", and the way in which the NAME is inseparably connected with the altar, the ark of the covenant, the cherubims, etc., furnishes proof of the truth of this statement.

The explanation of the symbology of the Holy of Holies and its furnishings, which shows wherein the power of the NAME consists, and how this power may really touch our lives on the three planes of our existence, transforming the race of men into something more than men, will be seen by careful, unprejudiced study of the following three chapters.

CHAPTER III

"Things Which Have Been Kept Secret from the Foundation of the World."
Matt. 13:35.

"The Lord is in his holy temple: let all the earth keep silence before him."
Hab. 2:20.

IT is a well-known fact that the Tabernacle in the Wilderness and Solomon's Temple typified the physical body of man. Jesus emphasized this symbol by inverting it, and calling his body the Temple, and similar references to our physical bodies as the temple of God are frequent throughout the New Testament. But these figures have not been generally comprehended at their full value. The significance of the Holy of Holies of the Tabernacle has been overlooked. Concerning this is "the mystery of God" (Rev. 10:7), "the mystery of Christ" (Col. 4:3), "the mystery which was kept secret since the world began" (Rom. 16:25), the things concerning which Moses gave testimony "which were to be spoken after" (Heb. 3:5).

Within the Holy of Holies we are told was put the ark of the covenant, or the ark of the testimony, whereupon was placed the mercy seat, which was overshadowed by the cherubims. The golden altar of incense was before the vail of the Holy of Holies. Complete accounts of the construction of the Tabernacle, with its laws and ordinances, are given in Exodus and Leviticus, but I would direct attention to Exodus 25:1–22 and to Leviticus 16:1–13, which furnish data for further study and comparison of references.

Naturally the symbology could not afford an exact counterbalance throughout, and still permit the erection of a usable, material structure for the Tabernacle, but a *thorough study* of the references relating to this subject throughout all parts of the Bible clearly shows what a superficial glance does not reveal—that the truth taught by the Holy of Holies, its furnishings and ordinances, the office of the high priest, the promises connected with the ark of the covenant and related references is that there is but one true mate for each soul; that the way out of human limitation—from man to superman—the way of eternal life of the body in youth and health, with its increasing refinement and rarification, is through the office of sex of such two individuals after their lives have become sufficiently spiritual by setting God first before their eyes, and by loving all humanity so much that by the natural working of the Law of Life they are reunited in a love so divinely pure and strong that it sees naught but God in all his handiwork.

The ark of the covenant, the mercy seat, the cherubims, etc., have reference to the female genitals; the altar of incense, the censer, etc. to those of the male. The cherubims are the labia majora: the censer is the phallus. The details of the analogy become apparent from the inter-relation. Aaron, the high priest, represents the male complement, who alone is permitted access to the Holy of Holies. Aaron's two sons (symbolical of his ideas or thoughts, hence of his resultant capacities or tendencies) Eleazar and Ithamar, who were to offer sacrifice continually with Aaron, typify by their names the qualities of pure love and spiritual understanding which Aaron must possess.

The sons of Aaron who were slain because they offered false fire upon the altar (Lev. 10:1–3) signify lack of self control, and a low understanding that grasps only the material phase of the sacrifice. These qualities must be slain in every man before he can become a high priest in this sense, which is "after the order of Melchizedek", who was said to be the priest of the Most High God long before there was any Jewish Liturgy in existence.

The very meagre reference to Melchizedek in the Bible makes it difficult for us to learn much about him, but it is recorded that he met Abraham when he was returning from the slaughter of the kings who had carried away Lot, and administered to him bread and wine, symbolical of the understanding of the Spirit, and of matter. We are also told that he was king of Salem, which is interpreted in the text as "King of Peace". While this would be true, this is not the first meaning of the word "Salem", which comes from a word meaning *whole*. Therefore we can judge that Melchizedek was one who possessed wholeness in its full significance by being in possession of the truth in regard to Spirit and matter, and related facts. Again, in the seventh chapter of Hebrews we read that Melchizedek's priesthood was a continual priesthood; that he was without "beginning of days" or "end of life", which corresponds to the truth with respect to the soul complement, which always has been and always will be the one to stand in the relation of high priest toward its true spiritual mate.

To those who may be inclined to treat lightly the idea that there exists a complement for every soul, let me say that this is no idle fancy adapted to satisfy the caprice of the giddy or frivolous, for one must be truly spiritual in his desires, and willing to give up anything that stands in the way of his finding God and doing the right before it is in his power to know the complement of his own soul, and the one of whom this is true will not be neglectful of duty nor inconsiderate of others.

This truth is the significance of the allegory related in Gen. 2:18–25. The incompleteness of the man without the woman is indicated by the woman's having been formed of a portion of the substance of the man's body, which it must be admitted is a very good figurative version of the biological facts referred to in Chapter V. Thus we see the thought expressed is that neither is complete without the other, the two being required for an integral being.

Again, this is plainly taught by Jesus' words to the Pharisees (Matt. 19 and Mark 10), the meaning of which has been entirely overlooked because of a wrong interpretation put upon his answer to the Sadducees (Matt. 22 and Mark 12). The Sadducees did not believe in the resurrection; therefore it is plain that their question was not asked with the honest purpose of securing information, but rather with the design to entangle Jesus by suggesting a situation which, as they thought, would necessarily arise in the event of a life after death, in such cases as that of the woman who had had seven husbands, which imaginary dilemma they evidently considered as conclusive proof that there could be no resurrection of the dead. But Jesus silenced this childish argument by letting them know that the institution of the cosmos is not governed by finite laws and customs, and told them plainly that "in heaven they neither *marry* nor are *given in marriage*, but are as the *angels of God* in heaven." But these words, which have been so narrowly construed, fall far short of saying that no true love relation can exist or be formed in heaven. They were only intended to cover the particular aspect of the subject of marriage with which the question of the Sadducees was concerned, and their force was directed to correct the impression that the conditions of earth must necessarily obtain in heaven, hence the plain statement that "in heaven they neither marry nor are given in marriage." But what we do have a right to infer from them (far from saying that there is no marriage in heaven) is that in the spiritual state existing in heaven, ceremonies and man-made laws are not necessary, but that this law of God which created them male and female in "the *beginning of the creation*", will adjust the true marriage.

The probabilities are that no one of the seven brothers who had as wife the woman in question was her real husband, but that in heaven, provided she has mastered life's lessons of love sufficiently, she would be united with her true mate. Otherwise, she would have to begin there just where she left off here and learn to love everyone and to forgive everyone before her spiritual powers would be sufficiently quickened for her to recognize her true mate.

That souls are created male and female is too plain for controversy from the references cited in Matthew and Mark. In the account in Mark Jesus says, in speaking of the bill of divorcement, "For the hardness of your heart he (Moses) wrote you this precept, but *from the beginning of the creation* God *made* them male and female. For this cause shall a man leave his father and mother and cleave to his wife; and they twain shall be one flesh: so then they are no more twain, but one flesh. What therefore *God* hath joined together let not man put asunder."

By careful reading the context shows that it was against the principle of the separation of what had been joined *from the beginning of the creation* to which Jesus particularly referred, for while he expressed no disapproval of Moses' granting them the privilege of divorce under certain conditions, the restrictions and limitations of which were designed to promote, on the whole, the highest development of humanity while it had not yet attained a sufficiently quickened spiritual consciousness for it to be possible for each to know his own true companion, yet he says, "But *from the beginning of the creation God made* them male and female," and implies that God joined particular male and female creations, for he adds, "What therefore *God* hath joined together let not man put asunder" although he had just previously signified his approval of Moses' action in allowing certain ones to be put asunder under the then existing state of enlightenment of mankind.

Now the force of this argument certainly would not fit the circumstances of ordinary life and marriage, because we know that God never joined "from the beginning of the creation" *any* two individuals united simply by an accepted marriage ceremony of this or any other age. Legal marriage ceremonies are being performed daily, but how could any of these be said to date "*from the beginning of the creation*"? Hence it is plain that the only male and female which *could* have been joined from the *beginning* would be those whom Jesus said God joined; in other words—dual parts of the same soul.

This establishes the fact that this masculine and feminine duality in unity is true between souls of *individuals* the same as it is true in the nature of *each* soul, and as we see by the meaning of the Holy Name, and observe in all forms of life, in the nature of God Himself. But since souls were created in the image of God, every completed (redeemed) soul must represent an individualized part of God, or the *power* of Two In One. Now it cannot be argued that this condition is wholly met in the male or female individual alone, else why male and female bodies instead of a uniform type of body among human beings, representing both elements? for our souls most certainly determine the form of our bodies.

Someone may say, "You have just said that each individual soul is masculine and feminine in nature; then why does not this satisfy the condition of a completed soul, created in the image of God, who is TWO IN ONE?" My answer is that although there *is a measure* of masculine capacity in woman and feminine capacity in man, these powers are not present in each in such proportion or manner as to constitute a completed individual, capable alone of reproduction, or of perfect equilibrium (rest and happiness), and evolution from man to superman. The feminine capacity in the soul of man is manifested in his body, in one particular, in the rudimentary male breast, but this cannot function. On the other hand, we know that the female breast could not function except through the intervention of masculine capacity. Now the soul capacity of individual man and woman is not complete unto itself any more than the individual bodies, but the perfected power of a completed soul created in the image of God—the power of the Two In One—rests only with true spiritual mates who have been willing to get so close to God that He has joined them again in eternal benediction, his overshadowing Spirit giving power to the union of their souls and bodies.

Jesus was indeed a mediator between God and man in the sense of teaching man that God is not some power *apart*, to whom offerings in a temple of wood or stone should be made as from an individual to a God who is *distinct* and *separate* from himself, but that man's *body* is the temple of the Living God, and the power of his teaching is destined sooner or later to uplift all mankind to where they can understand the mystery of the *Holy of Holies* of this temple of the *body*, and offer acceptable sacrifices therein.

The wisdom and efficacy of God's plan of creation and redemption of mankind is thus clearly seen in the endowment of the spiritual and physical faculties of which none are devoid—the desire for love and companionship (completion) that is within every soul; and its material concomitant, the cognizance of the presence of the Creative Life Energy in the physical body, the correct understanding of which will eventually, in one incarnation or another, cause every prodigal son to come to himself and say, "I will arise and go to my Father."

CHAPTER IV

SEARCH THE SCRIPTURES

"Unto the pure all things are pure."
Titus 1:15.

THERE may be some who will feel after having studied the passages cited and related references that this is not sufficient to establish the correctness of the interpretation which I have given of the Holy of Holies. Of such I would kindly ask not to form a hasty conclusion, but reserve any adverse opinion until you have read not only all of this volume, but the Bible itself from Genesis to Revelation with this interpretation in mind. I believe if you are honest with yourself, and are not hopelessly fettered by literalism, you will then agree with me that the purpose of the Bible is not simply to prepare us for death, but to bring us into our divine heritage with all that means here and now; to cause us to feel one with God at heart, and to bring us into possession of the paradise (not necessarily in a far away heaven but begun on earth made into heaven) which God has prepared for every soul when it is able to receive it by being made perfect in love, seeing God in all, and in this purity of thought putting away entirely from the life anything in which God may not be a sharer; and that the presentation of these truths which I am telling you in regard to the Holy of Holies and the Holy Name constitutes the substratum of the whole Bible.

This is the key to the proper interpretation of the Old Testament (and with this the New Testament is inseparably connected), as it is evident that its ethical value consists not in its biography, for the most part, nor in its history, the high points of which are woven into this marvelous collection of allegories, employed by the Old Testament writers or compilers as the parables were by Jesus, but in the deeper truth intended to be set forth in this manner, and in the cry of the prophets in the same figurative speech for the recognition of this truth, calling attention to the suffering and privation of all lands (characterized as the "wrath of God"), which exist in the world because of mankind's lack of knowledge of this truth, their blindness to the fact that God is all, and their neglect of the commandment: "Thou shalt have no other Gods before me."

It is written as though all that is recorded had taken place, but the truth is that while much of it did indeed take place, these incidents were used in the grand scheme of presenting to an awakening world the eternal verities of God—a story told to children, as it were, to point a moral—and instead of the law's having passed away, it has never yet been understood by the world in its true significance.

All this is not apparent, and we miss the value if we insist upon taking a literal interpretation, and disregard the fact that the purpose is to present in this form the simple truth concerning God and man and life; and that certain principles, capacities, qualities, and a record of the spiritual evolution of every individual and of mankind in general is represented by certain characters and incidents in their histories. We find it to be a repetition of the presentation of the same truths set forth in seeming historical record, and the fact that we know some of it to be accurate history, has constituted the blind to its deeper meaning, because history and allegory are so interwoven. But when we get the clue to its real purpose and its figurative style, we can see in it so plainly the evidences of a Supreme Wisdom that gave it to an undeveloped race in the form of sufficient fact admixed with the Eternal Truth itself to keep us digging through the clay and gravel while our spiritual senses were maturing to a point where we could appreciate the value of the truth in its purity when the subsoil should be reached, that we cannot avoid the conviction that the Bible has been preserved for us by an Over-ruling Love to teach the world a happier truth than it has ever dreamed, and because it is taught in the form of parable or myth in no wise detracts from its spiritual value.

St. Paul makes the definite statement that he regards the historical incidents of Abraham's life as allegorical. He says (Gal. 4:22–24): "For it is written that Abraham had two sons, the one by a bondmaid, the other by a free woman. But he who was of the bondwoman was born after the flesh; but he of the free woman was by promise. Which things are an allegory." The statement is plain and incontrovertible. In the revised version of 1881 the translators have made this read, "Which things *contain* an allegory." This is taking great liberty, and clouds the real meaning, for consulting the original text, we find the verb which they have translated "contain" is the present indicative of the verb "to be" and simply means "is". While the King James version puts this verb in the plural to obtain a smooth translation, it preserves the meaning perfectly. The word which is translated "allegory" in both cases is the declined form of the participle from the verb meaning "to allegorize" or "to speak allegorically". This is correctly used as a noun the same as the participle in English, so that an awkward rendering of the clause, but one which gives the true meaning would be, "Which is allegorizing" or "Which is (a) speaking allegorically."

And if the account be allegorical in this case, why not in most of the Old Testament history? The fact that the writers chose to use actual happenings in some instances, makes the narrative no less allegorical in the main. Nor does this in any measure lessen its spiritual value, but rather heightens it, for anyone who claims he can receive inspiration or uplift from a perusal of the greater part of the Old Testament history and biography, accepted literally, has certainly not advanced very far in the true Christian spirit.

And here let it be said that we are all too ready to reject, as containing no principle of truth, the myths and legends of other nations, overlooking the fact that some of the most valuable lessons of our own Bible are presented in the same manner. We know when Jesus said, "Behold a sower went forth to sow" he did not intend us to believe that he was relating an actual fact in regard to a farmer sowing his wheat or oats. This is as truly a myth as any, and yet we see its profound meaning from the interpretation which Jesus gave his disciples later.

The truth concerning God and man and nature is truth no matter in what way it may be presented. Different races and nations have different ways of expressing the same truth, but the Pharisees of every age are willing to reject the truth if presented to them through any other channel than the narrow grooves in which their minds have worked till they have all but lost the power of independent thought. If we regard all legend as containing no expression of truth, what shall we say of the 31st verse of the 38th Chapter of Job? "Canst thou bind the sweet influences of Pleiades, or loose the bands of Orion?" A certain legend in connection with these two constellations has reference to this same mystery of God.

Doubtless these myths and traditions were not, in their inception, intended to be understood to relate actual facts any more than the parables of our own Bible were so intended, but were merely made the vehicles of some phase of the simple truth concerning life, realized in ancient times by the spiritual teachers of the different nations, and clothed in this form to be kept alive and handed down from age to age. How the real truth involved could easily have become distorted, because only partially comprehended, and made the ground for abhorrent practices of later spiritually undeveloped adherents of certain forms of belief, can be readily understood by the record of the inhuman crimes included in the history of the growth and development of Christianity; the Inquisition, for instance; the Salem Witchcraft; all religious persecution, in fact, not to mention modern inconsistencies parading under the name of Christ Jesus and his teaching. We do not think of accusing Jesus of advocating this standard of conduct because certain ones professing to follow him were guilty of such unchristian acts. No more can we with certainty accuse the ancient teachers of other nations of degeneracy and folly because their followers, even including the priesthood, perhaps failed to comprehend the spirit and meaning of their teaching. And it must also be remembered that Christianity being the latest religion, humanity as a whole was naturally at a higher level when it was established than when the more ancient religions were founded, for as time goes on the world becomes more capable of comprehending and practising higher truth.

"That both the Assyrian and the Egyptian worship had a solid basis of truth is a fact to which the Bible itself bears this remarkable testimony:—'In that day shall Israel be the third with Egypt and with Assyria, even a blessing in the midst of the land;

whom the Lord of Hosts shall bless, saying, Blessed be Egypt my people, and Assyria the work of my hands, and Israel mine Inheritance' (Isaiah xix. 24).''

Know this, that truth is eternal. Jesus did not *make* truth, he taught it, and the wisdom of the Sages and the Wise Men of the East was no less wisdom because it existed in the world before Jesus' day. The truth ascribed to Moses, that had been given to the world centuries before Jesus' time, was comprehended by *some* great soul before Jesus came to interpret and re-establish it. For however or whenever the Levitical law came into existence, we know that Jesus knew the esoteric meaning of the outward form, and referred to this when he said that he came not to destroy the law but to fulfil it, and that one jot or tittle would not pass away until all be fulfilled; because the letter of the law was being fulfilled every day, and his whole life and teaching contradicted the idea of there being any efficacy in the ritualistic ceremony. The truth to which Jesus himself tells us that he came to *bear witness unto* was the *Eternal Truth* that was already in the world independent of his emphasizing it, and independent of any organized body of believers called "Christians"; and until men are broad enough and honest enough to acknowledge truth in whatever form it appears, they are only defrauding themselves by setting limits for their own advancement.

From the study of the following references and related texts, which can be traced in any good reference Bible, certain truths will be found to be set forth as clearly as is possible to be done by means of an institution which was both esoteric and exoteric. A systematic study of the whole Bible from this point of view would of course be more satisfactory, but we may form some idea of the far-reaching importance of the underlying truth typified by the Tabernacle and its ordinances from some few texts bearing directly on the subject.

It will be noticed by anyone studying the matter carefully that we have a rough outline of this truth (in symbolical terms, of course) included in the first three chapters of Genesis, carrying us forward to the present state of the race, where it must remain until the "mystery of God" has been made known and the "Son of Man revealed"; that is, excluded from the Garden of Eden, with the curse of hard labor to win his bread resting on the man, and sorrow and painful childbirth on the woman, until they "return unto the *ground*"—turn their attention to matter—learn what it is, conquer it, give it rightful recognition in the universal economy, and thus transform matter itself, until it ceases to be the heavy burden it now is, and our bodies becoming more rarified, absorb their needed nourishment from the air, doing away with the necessity of bread earned by toil; this latter being the truth symbolized by the pot of manna put into the ark of the covenant (Ex. 16:33–34 and Heb. 9:4).

Beginning with the 4th chapter of Genesis, it takes up the more lengthy task of developing the outline, giving repeated instances to emphasize the same truths under different circumstances. In this way we get a number of persons and places referring to the same general principle or thing, and we find the same truths set forth in greater detail as we proceed. For instance, Assyria, Egypt and Israel symbolize everywhere throughout the Bible the physical, mental and spiritual respectively; but other things also symbolize these *same* capacities or conditions. However, the reverse is not true—that a symbol signifies more than one thing except in the sense of a modification, enlargement or derivation from the one original idea. An example of this is water, which embraces the psychical realm, including mind, understanding, knowledge, etc. Babylon's significance is equivalent to that of Assyria, and the same is true of Tyre, as well as other places, and the evil associated with each is the evil of separation—that is, lack of unity with the mental and spiritual. But the passage quoted from Is. 19:24 shows that "in that day" (which is now dawning), Assyria, Egypt and Israel are to be made one with God's blessing.

To come to the texts referred to, the choice of the whole tribe of the Levites to minister unto Aaron, the High Priest of the House of Levi, and to keep the charge of the Tabernacle, but *not* before the tabernacle of witness, the altar, and the vessels of the sanctuary, teaches that no one can expect to be elevated to the office of high priest (be recognized by his true complement) until he is first a Levite (spiritually minded), or that the way of attainment toward the office of high priest is through spiritual development, as is seen from the thought in the following references:

"And I, behold I have taken the Levites from among the children of Israel instead of all the firstborn that openeth the matrix among the children of Israel: therefore the Levites shall be mine; Because all the firstborn are mine; for on the day that I smote all the firstborn in the land of Egypt, I hallowed unto me all the firstborn in Israel, both man and beast: mine shall they be: I am the Lord" (Num. 3:12–13).

"Take the Levites instead of all the firstborn among the children of Israel, and the cattle of the Levites instead of their cattle; and the Levites shall be mine; I am the Lord" (Num. 3:45).

"Then Moses stood in the gate of the camp, and said, Who is on the Lord's side? let him come unto me. And all the sons of *Levi* gathered themselves together unto him" (Ex. 32:26).

"And ye shall know that I have sent this commandment unto you, that my *covenant* might be with *Levi*, saith the Lord of hosts. My *covenant* was with *him* of life and peace;

and I gave them to him for the fear wherewith he feared me, and was afraid before my name. The law of truth was in his mouth, and iniquity was not found in his lips: he walked with me in peace and equity, and did turn many away from iniquity" (Mal. 2:4–6).

The truth that there is but one true mate for each soul is sufficiently evident from Jesus' teaching, and that the figure of Aaron answers to this need hardly be questioned. He stood the highest in privilege and authority with reference to the sanctuary. He alone was permitted to enter the Holy of Holies and offer sacrifice within the vail. It was Aaron's rod that budded which was to be laid up before the testimony to take away the murmurings of the children of Israel against Moses (for food and drink), and also that they *die* not. That is, with Aaron is the power to overcome hunger and death, for we read:

"And it shall come to pass that the man's rod, whom I shall choose, shall blossom: and I will make to cease from me the murmurings of the children of Israel, whereby they murmur against you. . . . And it came to pass that on the morrow Moses went into the tabernacle of witness; and, behold, the rod of Aaron for the house of *Levi* was budded and brought forth buds, and bloomed blossoms, and yielded almonds.... And the Lord said unto Moses, Bring Aaron's rod again before the testimony, to be kept for a token against the rebels; and thou shalt quite take away their murmurings from me that they *die* not" (Num. 17:5, 8, 10).

"And the Lord said unto Aaron, Thou and thy sons and thy father's house with thee shall bear the iniquity of the sanctuary: and thou and thy sons with thee shall bear the iniquity of your priesthood. And thy brethren also of the tribe of Levi, the tribe of thy father, bring thou with thee, that they may be joined unto thee, and minister unto thee; but thou and thy sons with thee shall minister before *the tabernacle of witness*. And they shall keep thy charge and the charge of all the tabernacle: only they shall *not* come nigh the vessels of the sanctuary and the altar, that neither *they*, nor *ye* also, *die*.... And *ye* shall keep the charge of the *sanctuary* and the charge of the *altar*: that there be no wrath any more upon the children of Israel.

Therefore thou and thy sons with thee shall keep your priest's office for everything of the altar, and *within* the vail; and ye shall serve: I have given your priest's office unto you as a service of *gift*: and the *stranger* that cometh nigh shall be put to death" (Num. 18:1–3, 5, 7).

The stranger represents anyone who is not the true complement, and being *put to death* is intended in the deeper significance to refer to dying just as mankind has always done. The fact that as long as *strangers* come nigh the sanctuary mankind will continue to die is again emphasized in these words:

"And thou shall appoint Aaron and his sons, and they shall wait on their priest's office: and the *stranger* that cometh nigh shall be *put to death*. . . . But those that encamp before the Tabernacle toward the east, even before the Tabernacle of the Congregation eastward, shall be Moses and Aaron and his sons, keeping the charge of the sanctuary for the charge of the children of Israel; and the *stranger* that cometh nigh shall be *put to death*" (Num. 3:10, 38).

This is certainly intended to call our attention forcibly to the fact that anyone but the true complement has not the power to overcome death.

Referring again to "Bible Mystery and Bible Meaning", the author states in the first chapter:

"The Bible is the Book of the Emancipation of Man. The emancipation of man means his deliverance from sorrow and sickness, from poverty, struggle and uncertainty, from ignorance and limitation, and finally from death itself. This may appear to be what the euphuistic colloquialism of the day would call 'a tall order', but nevertheless it is impossible to read the Bible with a mind unwarped by antecedent conceptions derived from traditional interpretation without seeing that this is exactly what it promises, and that it professes to contain the secret whereby this happy condition of perfect liberty may be attained. Jesus says that if a man keeps his saying he shall never see death (John 8:51): in the Book of Job we are told that if a man has with him 'a messenger, an interpreter', he shall be delivered from going down to the pit, and shall return to the days of his youth (Job 33:24): the Psalms speak of our renewing our youth (Ps. 103:5):

and yet again we are told in Job that by acquainting ourselves with God we shall be at peace, we shall lay up gold as dust and have plenty of silver, we shall decree a thing and it shall be established unto us (Job 22:21–23). . . .

"The first thing to notice is that there is a common element running through the texts I have quoted; they all contain the idea of acquiring certain information, and the promised results are all contingent on our getting this information and using it. Jesus says it depends on our keeping his saying, that is, receiving the information which he had to give and acting upon it. Job says that it depends on rightly interpreting a certain message, and again that it depends on our making ourselves acquainted with something; and the context of the passage in Psalms makes it clear that the deliverance from death and the renewal of youth there promised are to be attained through the 'ways' which the Lord 'made known unto Moses'."

It is interesting to note how all of this, though unwittingly on the part of the author, points directly to the information which I am telling you lies buried in the symbology of the Pentateuch.

Further reference to eternal life we find in Deut. 4:40:

"Thou shalt keep therefore his statutes and his commandments, which I command thee this day, that it may go well with thee and with thy children after thee, and that thou mayest prolong thy days *upon the earth*, which the Lord thy God giveth thee, *for ever*.": and in Hosea 13:14:

"I will ransom them from the power of the *grave*; I will redeem them from *death*: O death, I will be thy plagues; O grave, I will be thy destruction: repentance shall be hid from mine eyes."

We also read that this salvation and everlasting strength is in the Lord JEHOVAH. The original text must have been strongly emphasized in some way to cause the translators to put the word "Jehovah" in large capitals thus:

"Behold God is my salvation; I will trust and not be afraid: for the Lord JEHOVAH is my strength and my song; he also is become my salvation" (Is. 12:2).

"Trust ye in the Lord forever: for in the

Lord JEHOVAH is *everlasting strength*" (Is. 26:4).

This links the power of the Holy Name "YEVE" with the prosperity and eternal life to which our attention has been called, and we also find the NAME of the Lord associated with the symbology of the temple and the ark of the covenant in the following references:

"And David arose and went with all the people that were with him from Baale of Judah, to bring up from thence the ark of God, whose name is called by the *name of the Lord of hosts* that dwelleth between the cherubims" (2 Sam. 6:2).

"If, when evil cometh upon us, as the sword, judgment or pestilence, or famine, we stand before this house, and in *thy presence* (for thy *name* is in this house), and cry unto thee in our affliction, then thou wilt hear and help" (2 Chr. 20:9).

Note the force of Deut. 12:11 in connection with Is. 37:16:—

"Then there shall be a place which the Lord your God shall choose to cause his *name* to dwell there; thither shall ye bring all that I command you; your burnt offerings and your sacrifices, your tithes and the heave offering of your hand, and all your *choice vows* which ye vow unto the Lord."

"O Lord of hosts, God of Israel, that dwellest between the cherubims, thou art the God, even thou alone, of all the kingdoms of the earth: thou hast made heaven and earth."

By Genesis 3:24 we learn that without knowledge of this truth we cannot be granted entrance back into the garden of Eden (freedom from suffering and limitation), for we are told:

"He drove out the man; and he placed at the *east* of the garden of Eden cherubims and a flaming sword which turned *every way* to keep the way of the tree of life." That is, this truth being the most *unsuspected* and the last to be rightly comprehended, would naturally include a right understanding of other related truths necessary to be understood, such as the right conception of matter, and a knowledge of the spiritual significance of the relation between male and female. The latter statement is the truth emphasized in Malachi 2:13–15:

"And this have ye done again, covering the altar of the Lord with tears, with weeping and with crying out, insomuch that he regardeth not the offering any more, or receiveth it with good will at your hand. Yet ye say, Wherefore? (The answer follows.) Because the Lord hath been witness between thee and the *wife of thy youth*, against whom thou hast dealt treacherously: yet is she thy *companion* and the wife of thy *covenant*. And did he not *make one*? Yet had he the residue of the spirit. And wherefore *one*? (Again the answer.) That he might seek a *godly seed*. Therefore take heed to your *spirit* and let none deal treacherously against the wife of his youth."

This passage has been interpreted to mean nothing more than an admonition against divorce or unfaithfulness to any wedded companion, but in the light of the whole truth it seems far more reasonable that "the *wife of thy covenant*", and "*the wife of thy youth*" refers, in its deepest significance, to the one *joined* to the true husband *from the beginning*, and that this is the information that we were intended eventually to get out of it. As long as we were unaware that there is such a mate, naturally we would not see this meaning in it, and it serves its first purpose by inculcating the lesson of faithfulness and kindliness, but this is an example of God's method, through the instrument of the prophet, of opening our eyes to the full truth, through the only means which lifts man from lower to higher—the *putting into practice* the law of conduct nearest to the truth of which he may at any time have knowledge.

The question, "And did he not *make one*?" "And wherefore *one*?" strongly suggests this; and the answer, "That he might seek a *godly seed*" is shown to be the means of removing the "*curse*" mentioned in verses 1–4 of this same chapter:

"And now, ye priests, this commandment is for you. If ye will not hear, and if ye will not *lay it to heart* to give glory unto my *name* saith the Lord of hosts, I will even send a *curse* upon you, and I will curse your blessings: yea, I *have* cursed them already, because ye do not *lay it to heart*. (Note the force of that sentence referring to the figurative "wrath of God".) Behold I will *corrupt your seed*, and spread dung upon your faces, even the dung of your solemn feasts; and one shall take you away with it. And ye shall know that I have sent this commandment unto you, that my *covenant* might be with *Levi*, saith the Lord of hosts." In other words, all the blessings promised under the covenant (the release from suffering and limitation) can only be possible when the right conditions have been established; that is, when the high priest (who was always of the house of Levi under the ceremonial law) is the only one to offer sacrifices. This is the true monogamy. This is the real science of eugenics.

If anyone still doubts the interpretation put upon the sacrifices and offerings, study without prejudice Lev. 21:16–23.

"And the Lord spake unto Moses, saying, Speak unto Aaron, saying, Whosoever he be of thy seed in their generations that hath any blemish, let him not approach to offer the bread of his God. For whatsoever man he be that hath a blemish, he shall not approach: a blind man or a lame, or he that hath a flat nose, or anything superfluous, or a man that is brokenfooted, or brokenhanded, or crookbackt, or a dwarf, or that hath a blemish in his eye, or be scurvy or scabbed, or hath his stones broken; No man that hath a blemish of the seed of Aaron the priest shall come nigh to *offer* the offerings of the Lord made by fire: he hath a blemish; he shall not come nigh to offer the bread of his God. He shall eat the bread of his God, both of the most holy and of the holy. Only he shall not go *in unto the vail*, nor come nigh unto the altar because he hath a blemish; that he profane not my sanctuaries: for I the Lord do sanctify them.

Why should a priest be denied particularly the privilege to go *in unto the vail*, or to *offer* an offering by fire because he was deformed, if this refers to nothing but ceremony and ritual? It should be plain to anyone that this is intended to preclude deformed persons from physical union effective for procreation for the sake of the race.

In explanation of certain passages that have a general bearing on the subject, we find that Jacob and Esau represent the spiritual and material powers of man, regardless of Jacob's deplorable trickery in many instances; and the line, "Jacob have I loved, but Esau have I hated" I think to be as inadequately translated as the saying of Jesus that if a man came to him and *hated* not his mother and father, etc. he could not be his disciple. While there is apparently but one meaning given for the verb "miseo", which is the word used in both the New Testament references, we know it must have had a different significance than our word "hate", for we know that Jesus never intended to teach that we should hate our father or mother or anyone for any cause, since this is the exact antithesis of the spirit of his teaching. In this we have an example of where the "anointing of the Spirit" teaches us better than the written word itself, which is equally true of many other passages which may be taken too literally.

There are various instances in Jacob's biography where the literal record has no moral uplift, but when we remember that it is merely a story to illustrate certain facts, we need not concern ourselves so much with the device used as with the facts it is intended to point out. It was necessary to frame some kind of excuse for Jacob's getting the birthright although he was slightly younger than Esau, for the truth involved in this instance is that the spiritual powers of man are destined to rule over the material, even though developed later, as we have our bodies and physical senses before our spiritual life is awakened. Again, the instance of Jacob's method of increasing the share of the flocks that was to be his, which was as unprincipled as actual stealing, is intended to teach the tremendous truth of the effect on physical substance of thought during sexual congress.

As we follow Jacob's career, we find it to represent the spiritual evolution of an individual toward the realization of the full truth. When he wrestles with the angel, he is struggling with the problem of the right relation of Spirit and matter, which is a corollary to the truth hidden in the meaning of the Holy Name. Then we read of the reconciliation of Jacob and Esau—Spirit and matter—with all that this implies.

The twelve sons of Jacob, the heads of the tribes of Israel, represent the capacities or powers of an individual in their mental or spiritual, and physical inter-relation. If anyone thinks I am simply making an arbitrary statement to suit my own purpose, then answer what Jesus meant when he said, "Verily I say unto you that ye which have followed me in the regeneration, when the Son of Man shall sit in the throne of his glory, ye also shall sit upon twelve thrones, judging the twelve tribes of Israel" (Matt. 19:28). Do you think he meant us to accept that literally? He was using symbolical language as he did constantly in his teaching.

Of these twelve sons, Joseph refers to the sex function in its purity and spiritual reality. His being sold into Egypt, which symbolizes mental faculty or mind alone, independent of spiritual understanding, represents our blindness to the facts in connection with the faculty typified by Joseph on account of our incomplete conception of the truth. Joseph's children, Ephraim and Manasseh, represent the same thing only more specifically, Ephraim signifying the spiritual reality and Manasseh the physical. Here again we find the instance of the younger (spiritual) receiving the blessing of the birthright over the elder (material), for it is recorded that Jacob "wittingly" guided his hands and placed his *right* hand upon the head of Ephraim, and his *left* on that of Manasseh when blessing Joseph's children (Gen. 48).

Judah represents our ethical and spiritual

promptings—our wish to do the right and shun the wrong—even though our understanding of right and wrong be imperfect.

David stands for the perfected spiritual understanding in man, or the all conquering kingdom of the Spirit, to which all other powers, mental and physical, must eventually render obedience. He represents the power of the right relation of body, mind and Spirit, his stronghold of defense being the power of sex uplifted. This explains the meaning of the expression, "the *key* of the house of David" (Is. 22:22). Besides being represented as king, David is also spoken of as shepherd because of his spiritual understanding of the creative energy (the Christos), which he exemplifies, and which is the power that will, in the end, bring the last wandering sheep back to the Father's fold. In Ezekiel 34:23 we read: "And I will set up one shepherd over them, and he shall feed them, even my servant David; he shall feed them, and he shall be their shepherd."

For this reason any exponent of this whole truth of God concerning the union of Spirit and matter in our bodies, whether Joseph, David or Jesus, is spoken of as the shepherd.

This power is also referred to as the stone of stumbling, because of the deep mystery of God which it holds, and over it we continually stumble until we can view it from the spiritual aspect; then the "key of the house of David" unlocks the mystery. We find such reference to Joseph in Gen. 49:22–24:

"Joseph is a fruitful bough, even a fruitful bough by a well; whose branches run over the wall: The archers have sorely grieved him, and shot at him and hated him. But his bow abode in strength, and the arms of his hands were made strong by the hands of the mighty God of Jacob; (from thence is the *shepherd*, the *stone of Israel*:)"

This is the stone which the builders of the temple have always despised. Jesus' reference to this is proof of its application to this interpretation: "Did ye never read in the scriptures, The stone which the builders rejected, the same is become the head of the corner: This is the *Lord's* doing and it is marvelous in our eyes?" What would be marvelous about it in our eyes because it was the *Lord's* doing, if it were not something that our immature understanding had led us to believe would *not* be the Lord's doing?

But this is because the "Judah" in each one of us is the lawgiver first, and when all is said, this is just the way God ordered it. We all have to come through this same experience of shock when this deeper truth of God is borne in upon us. But we are told that Judah and Joseph (or Ephraim, which means the same), are to become one.

"Moreover, thou son of man, take thee one stick, and write upon it, For Judah, and for the children of Israel his companions: then take another stick, and write upon it, For Joseph, the stick of Ephraim, and for all the house of Israel his companions: And join them one to another into one stick; and they shall become one in thine hand" (Ezekiel 37:16–17). And it is then we can look upon this matter as God sees it.

If there still remains a shadow of doubt in anyone's mind as to the accuracy of my premises—the certainty that by the Holy of Holies with its furnishings, the ark of the covenant, the tabernacle of witness, or merely the tabernacle in some instances, with the associated sacrifices and offerings, are really meant the organs of reproduction, their functions, etc., then I shall be obliged to call his attention to Lev. 15:31–33, where the instance given of the defiling of God's tabernacle among us is *not* veiled, and to Is. 57:7, where the prophet has interpreted his own symbol. But let all men *beware* of thinking as " natural brute beasts" because the most sacred things of God are thus associated with our physical bodies that the physical feature has the same power as the spiritual attitude, and mark *well* what I say in regard to the right spiritual conditions in the following chapters.

It is because we have thought that matter is no part of God, and consequently that it would not be possible for this bodily function to be so closely associated with the Spirit of God, that we have had wrong thoughts about it, and have made it an obstacle to the attainment of our highest life in God. On this account we have wanted to be sure that our will to control every part of our bodies would not be enslaved by any desire, and this is right; it is just as God intended it to be, for in this new understanding of this function the primary emphasis is on perfect control before we are in a position to use it rightly. This control is one of the qualities developed under the standard of Judah, and we are told in Gen. 49:10, "The scepter shall not depart from Judah, nor a lawgiver from between his feet, until Shiloh come; and unto him shall the gathering of the people be." After we have learned control to the point of sacrificing anything upon the altar of devotion to our highest ideals of right, then God checks that lesson off, as it were, and goes back to take up another phase of our education to teach us that He is all and in all, and to remove some of the impressions that had to be a little overdrawn in the first place to cause us to get the point intended, and a new lesson is assigned, the idea of which we get from the following references:

"A son honoureth his father, and a servant his master: If then I be a father, where is mine honour? and if I be a master, where is my fear? saith the Lord of hosts unto you, O priests, that despise my *name*. And ye say, *Wherein* have we despised thy *name*? (Answer.) Ye offer *polluted bread* upon mine altar; and ye say, *Wherein* have we polluted thee? (Answer.) In that ye say, The table of the Lord is *contemptible*" (Mal. 1:6–7).

(In this mention of "the *table* of the Lord" we again find the same thought as that suggested by the pot of manna put into the ark of the covenant.)

"I have spread out my hands all the day unto a rebellious people, which walketh in a way that was not good, after their *own* thoughts; A people that provoketh me to anger continually to my face; that *sacrificeth in gardens*, and burneth incense upon altars of *brick*;.... Which say (Speaking to God!) Stand by *thyself*, come not *near* to *me*; for I am *holier* than *thou*. These are a smoke in my nose, a fire that burneth all the day" (Is. 65:2, 3, 5).

"Shall the work say of him that *made* it, He made me *not*? Or shall the thing *framed* say of him that *framed* it, He had no *understanding*?" (Is. 29:16).

"Shall mortal man be more just than God? shall a man be more *pure* than his maker?" (Job 4:17).

Because Ephraim hath made many altars to sin, altars shall be unto him to sin. I have *written* to him the *great* things of my *law*, but they were counted as a *strange* thing. They sacrifice *flesh* for the sacrifices of mine offerings, and *eat* it; but the Lord accepteth them not;.... For Israel hath forgotten his maker and *buildeth* temples (Hosea 8:11–14).

"Howbeit the most High dwelleth *not* in temples made with *hands* as saith the prophet, Heaven is my throne, and earth is my footstool: what house will ye build me? saith the Lord: or what is the place of my rest? Hath not my hand made *all these things*? Ye stiff necked and uncircumcised in *heart* and *ears*, ye do always resist the Holy Ghost: as your fathers did, so do ye" (Acts. 7:48–51).

"For *my* thoughts are not *your* thoughts, neither are *your* ways *my* ways, saith the Lord" (Is. 55:8).

"Know ye not that *ye* are the temple of God, and that the Spirit of God dwelleth in you? If any man defile the temple of God, him shall God destroy; for the temple of God is holy, which temple *ye* are" (1 Cor. 3:16–17).

But even the Master Himself had to learn this truth concerning the Holy of Holies of this temple of the body ere he realized his full mission. It should be borne in mind that the name of Jesus has a significance similar to the name "Jehovah". My authority for this statement is the late Richard Francis Weymouth, M.A., D.Lit., Fellow of University College (London), Editor of "The Resultant Greek Testament" and author of the "New Testament in Modern Speech". I quote from the "New Testament in Modern Speech", p. 4 (Third Edition), Note 4: ". . . . The full significance of the name 'Jesus' is seen in the original 'Yeho-Shua', which means 'Jehovah the Saviour', and not merely 'saviour', as the word is commonly explained." Thus Christ's mission is indicated by the meaning of his name, which we see to be associated with the Holy Name. But we are told that even he was made perfect through suffering, to which there is ample reference; one in the symbolical statement in Rev. 11:8. This passage alone should be sufficient to disillusion any who feel they must put a literal interpretation upon all parts of the Bible. I repeat that the Bible is an admixture of historical fact with the symbolical teaching of this mystery of the higher truth, which has thus been preserved. This has given the Bible its wide circulation, and will cause it to endure through all time. We know Christ *was not* crucified in Sodom or Egypt, as here stated, except in the sense indicated by these symbols. And with these facts accord the words attributed to Jesus, discovered only in recent years: "Let not him who seeks cease until he finds, and when he finds he shall wonder, and wondering he shall reach the Kingdom, and having reached the Kingdom he shall rest."

CHAPTER V

THE FIRE OF THE LORD

TO review in brief some of the facts already mentioned, it is as if the soul, as we ordinarily use the term, is but a partial expression of a soul that in the beginning was a complete embodiment of masculine and feminine power, but that the Creative Law, when investing this soul with physical form in which to work out its experiences, gain the mastery over evil (which is equivalent to gaining a right conception of the truth in all its phases), and the capacity for unending happiness, gave portions of the soul separate bodies at an early stage in the evolutionary process, endowing both with certain similar capacities and certain complementary ones.

The science of zoology supports this opinion in the like development of the physical organism through asexual and hermaphrodite stages toward the separate sexes. In the branch Protozoa we find forms of life that are asexual and reproduce by fission, budding, etc. In the next higher branch—Poriferata—we find in certain varieties of the sponges the appearance of separate male and female reproductive cells, but combined in one body. Ascending through the various orders of the higher branches, we see the male and female cells becoming more distinct in structure; in some cases, as for instance the Portuguese Man-of-War, both pedunculated, yet belonging to the one organism, until finally in the still higher branches they appear in separate bodies.

I realize the analogy is not complete, as the ascent from the branch Protozoa is more lateral than lineal; that is, the sponge, is a completed animal in its branch, having advanced along a path parallel to, we might say, but not necessarily identical with the animals of the higher branches; the same being true of the Portuguese Man-of-War. Nevertheless, these are examples of forms of animal life still existing, which furnish the clue to the evolutionary trend—the general course over which man has ascended to his higher goal from the particular protoplasmic cell, the quality and nature of which I hold the

Creator must have *designed* to produce a human being.

If any doubt the judgment of the scientist concerning the mute testimony of the past ages regarding the facts of evolution, then let him listen with reason and honesty to the ceaseless repetition of the record of the development of the human being through lower forms of life and undifferentiated sex, by a living witness whose verity cannot be questioned—the human embryo. But to accept the facts of evolution as true does not necessitate the acceptance of the materialistic theory as to the *cause* of these facts, as seems to be the general impression. It is the erroneous conclusions of physical science, which overlook God as the intelligence back of the evolutionary plan that cause a great many people who have made no particular effort to inform themselves on the subject, to disbelieve actual facts as well as this theory. For most people instinctively feel, and rightly so, that there is something radically wrong with the cheerless doctrine that all life and attainment are the results of the action of mechanical causes upon inert matter. But this mistaken theory, deduced from observations which establish the physical facts, comes from not consulting spiritual as well as material evidence as to the meaning of the facts.

It is the combined use of reason and intuition that enables us to draw right conclusions from any given data. The materialistic scientist who disregards the voice of intuition is no more to blame, however, than the moralist who disregards the voice of reason. Neither is quite honest. For the moralist to declare that he does not want to be convinced of any given fact lest his faith in God's love and goodness should be shaken, is to admit that he is willing to be hoodwinked and live in a fool's paradise. We need never be afraid to have the changeless, eternal truth uncovered, and the greater measure of truth we comprehend, the more plainly do we see the happy goal toward which all things are tending.

To fail to listen to intuition, which always associates our existence with a loving Father, is to limit our aspirations and happiness because of the gloomy philosophy deduced from physical facts alone. Likewise, to fail to listen to reason as to the existence of these facts also limits our aspirations and happiness because of the narrowing effect it has upon our outlook upon life, and the check it puts upon advancement and expansion in all directions, due to the failure to believe as possible the developments and attainments foreshadowed in the facts themselves when rightly interpreted as to cause and trend.

In regard to the physical form, science tells us that the evolution of our hermaphrodite ancestors resulted in the dual expression of male and female human beings. This being true, we must, in the light of advancing knowledge, also concede a cleavage of the original soul capacity, which wrought the subsequent selection of the distinct masculine and feminine reproductive physical substance and forms, by the respective masculine and feminine complementary elements of mind and soul. For if the physical forms of our early invertebrate ancestors, and possibly the lowest vertebrate, were hermaphrodite, and the separation of the sexes took place through division of labor, the conclusion is unavoidable that when certain physical functions were apportioned for obtaining better results, the corresponding psychical elements must also at the same time have been selected from the total by both evolving individuals for performing their particular duties. This at least establishes the reasonableness of a theory which at first thought might seem wholly fanciful or unfounded.

And it would seem in the case of the man and woman possessing parts of the same soul, that the power of recognition of each other had been placed so deep within that they are obliged to learn the lessons of life which develop their spiritual senses, and to seek the Spirit within themselves before they can regain this power of recognition which was wholly lost to them while living in either the physical or mental state of consciousness. Before they are sufficiently developed spiritually, they must have a genuine unselfish love for all humanity—a love that seeks to serve at every opportunity—and before they can know without doubt or misgiving the complement of their own souls, the dross of all impurity of thought must have been purged away to such extent that God can be recognized as all, and all as God.

It should be remembered that the principle

sex means more than physical sex organs and passion. The underlying reality which finds ultimate expression in the physical bodies of individuals, is the principle of the positive and negative forces of the Universal Life Energy, which has brought all organized forms into existence from the compounds of mineral atoms to man.

This same upward drawing Power which works through every individual life, causing it to evolve from lower to higher physically, mentally and spiritually, is, in the language of Scripture, the Christos; literally, "the anointed": hence one chosen for a special service. After creating and perfecting physical forms of life, its service now is to establish the universal consciousness that God is ONE; that the universal substance is a manifestation of the Absolute as truly as is the Spirit which pervades it; that certain elements of this substance vibrating at a rate sufficiently slow to be perceptible to the physical senses, or what we speak of as physical matter, is also God, and that every natural function of our physical bodies was made to be perfected until God can be glorified through it. This is the Power which has inspired the spiritual leaders and seers of all ages and nations, which was personified by David and was incarnate in the man Jesus.

It is this principle, which was manifested in greater measure in Jesus than in any other, instead of the man Jesus himself, that we should bear in mind to read understandingly either the Old or the New Testament. We know that Jesus did not refer to his own personality when he said, "I am the way, the truth and the life: no man cometh unto the Father but by me." Again, he says plainly, "He that believeth on me, believeth not on me, but on him that sent me" (John 12:44). This meaning of the Creative Life Principle, or Christos, is made plain in Micah 5:2: "But thou, Bethlehem Ephratah, though thou be little among the thousands of Judah, yet out of thee shall he come forth unto me that is to be ruler in Israel; whose goings forth have been *from of old, from everlasting*."

This Creative Energy operates through all our talents and capacities, but its stronghold for transforming the matter of which our bodies are composed, and for purifying our minds from misconceptions of the truth in regard to all of God's universe is the sex power in its twofold physical and spiritual significance, enabling us at length to see that all is God. The working of the Christos through the sex centers on the substance which constitutes our material bodies is the fire of the Lord, so often mentioned in the Bible. This is the import of John's statement that Christ would baptize with the Holy Ghost and with fire; that is with such power of spiritual discernment as enables one to see the Father in all his work, even in this effect upon our physical bodies, which it becomes very evident upon study, means a combination of *electrical* and *spiritual* power so closely united as to be inseparable.

Our attention is first called to this fact by the allegorical account of Moses' face *shining* when he comes down from the mount, and the many references to thunder and *lightning* about the mount, which holy mountain also refers to the place of the sanctuary. This evidence of the presence of electricity is supplemented by the record of Ezekiel's vision in the first chapter of Ezekiel.

To better understand the strange imagery

of this chapter, which is a setting forth of the most sacred and profound truths of God's creation, let us note first the meaning of some of the symbols employed as they are commonly used throughout the Bible. Pure Spirit is represented by light, the color white and wind. The action of Spirit on matter is represented by fire. Ezekiel mentions the fact that the whirlwind came out of the *north*. This is significant because the names of the four directions have weighty meanings in symbolical language, as do the signs of the Zodiac, as anciently associated with familiar facts of life. The north, which is associated with the sign of the Bull (or ox), champions the working out of spiritual conceptions in matter, hence the bodily union of man and woman. Without the qualities symbolized by this sign we should be impractical, incapable of accomplishing things in the material world. In its lower aspect (separated from its spiritual reality, for this alone is what constitutes the lower aspect of any capacity of mind or body), it genders anger, strife and lust; uplifted through spiritual discernment, it begets strength and pure, ardent love and becomes the chief avenue for the action of the Christos on the substance of our bodies—the means of their further evolution toward refinement, rarification and eternal existence, through transformation.

The East, associated with Scorpio, and the Eagle (which means Scorpio uplifted), champions the soul union of man and woman in a love by which they are made one through the Christ consciousness, whereby the sex force is discovered to be what it is in its spiritual reality, and thus becomes uplifted.

The South, associated with the man, or angel, champions the kindly, passionless mother love that enfolds all the world in its yearning sympathy.

The West, associated with the Lion, champions integrity, uprightness, and high purpose, with a suggestion of severity in its devotion to duty. From an abnormal development of these qualities by themselves we should get narrow mindedness, religious intolerance, etc., but rightly balanced, are summed up in purity and moral courage.

Now the qualities of no one of these signs are sufficient of themselves. The Creator did not intend it to be so, and the reign of the "kings" mentioned by Daniel, which come forth in solitary power from any of these directions, is characterized by evil. It requires the blending of all four into one for the desired resultant—the high spiritual understanding that puts the proper value upon matter, sees it as a worthy servant—the medium for the expression of the life of the Spirit—and by this understanding and use of it, transforms and spiritualizes matter itself.

Returning again to the first appearance of the vision, our attention is called to the action of Spirit on matter by the presence of the whirlwind and the fire. The significance of the whirlwind's coming from the *north* has been explained. From the description of the living creatures we see (verse 7) that their feet resembled calves' feet (in significance those of the ox), and that they sparkled like the color of burnished brass. By verse 10 we learn that they all had four faces (powers of recognition)—the face of a man, a lion, an ox and an eagle. It would take us too far afield to speak here of every minute detail mentioned, which in interpreting symbols must not be overlooked, but as an example, notice the position of those four faces. The faces of the man and the lion were on the *right* side, and the face of the ox on the *left* side. He does not definitely locate the face of the eagle. This is also significant as we shall presently see. How odd they must have looked! Their delineation would rival a specimen of futurist art; but it must be borne in mind that the "living creatures" were just an assemblage of symbolical entities to indicate the qualities necessary to produce the super-man, who will be aware of and able to appropriate his inherent power of endless life.

We have already called attention to the meaning and position of the four faces; but what is the force of the fact that the faces of the man and the lion were on the right side? The right side symbolizes the initiative power of pure Spirit, while the left represents the stabilizing power of matter, which together show forth the complete being of God (the Absolute, who manifests as both Spirit and matter as we ordinarily use the terms) in the proper union of Spirit and matter. Notice that the qualities of the man and the lion are those of the soul and Spirit only, while those of the ox have to do with matter, hence that face is on the left side. It is of singular interest that he does not tell us where the face of the eagle is. It would not be consistent for it to be on either the exact right or left, for while the capacity symbolized by the eagle has to do with matter in the sense of discovering its rightful place and lifting it up, it is a quality of soul or Spirit that is above and independent of matter in its initiative action.

To go back a little, why was the preference given to the ox that there should be both a face and feet of this type? Because among the divine realities of existence which are focused in and expressed through the physical body of man, the feet represent the understanding, in the sense of a correct mental comprehension, the hearing representing spiritual perception. This explains the meaning of Jesus' act in washing the disciples' feet—cleansing the understanding. And before man can become anything more than he now is, it is necessary to have a better understanding in regard to the qualities indicated by the sign of the ox, which have been stated in connection with the meaning of the directions, as we already possess a clearer understanding of the value of the capacities indicated by the other signs than we have had of this. The fact that they were the feet of a young animal shows that it was the most recently acquired knowledge, or the last necessary to begin the perfecting of man. The significance of the fact that they sparkled like burnished brass is in the particular kind of metal mentioned. The language of symbolism is marvelously concise and expressive, and we may look for special meanings in seemingly trivial details. Why were the feet of *brass* instead of gold or silver, for instance? In the analysis of the facts in regard to this point we again find reference to electricity, for brass, as we know, is an alloy of copper and zinc—the metals used to generate electricity in a simple cell. Bear in mind that the knowledge possessed by certain of the ancients, concerning the hidden forces and laws of Nature will afford work of investigation for modern science for some time to come. The *brass feet*, therefore, indicate that it is necessary that we *understand* the scientific and physiological purpose and explanation of the law of physical union championed by the ox, and that its nature and possibilities are *electrical*.

Coming to verses 13 and 14, we again find this repeated mention of *lightning*, further emphasizing the presence of electricity in connection with this fire of the Lord. The truth that furnishes the key to the higher evolution of the race is contained in verses 16–21 of this chapter, and in verses 9–17 of the 10th chapter, referring to the movements of the living creatures. In the 10th chapter, Ezekiel relates having seen the same vision as the one described with the exception that the face of the cherub was seen instead of the face of the ox. He takes particular care to tell us that it is identically the same living creature, and the presence of the cherub (equivalent to the cherubim) is wholly consistent. Please read both chapters carefully.

In regard to the figure of the wheel so often referred to, this word "wheel" is translated elsewhere in the margin as "whirling dust". Here again we find the same idea as expressed by the whirlwind and the fire, mentioned in the 4th verse of the 1st chapter—the action of Spirit (symbolized by the wind), on matter, for he tells us the appearance of the wheel was like unto the color of a beryl. Now a beryl may be either green or yellow, but evidently the yellow (flame-colored) beryl is meant here. Now look at the 13th verse of the 10th chapter: "As for the wheels, it was cried unto them in my hearing, O wheel." For the wheel to be thus addressed suggests the presence of a living intelligence, indicating that the very Spirit of Life Itself is inseparably connected with this action of the Spirit on matter, which is apparently just what the prophet is trying to impress upon us when he recounts in so many ways the movements of the creatures:

"And when the living creatures went, the wheels went by them: and when the living creatures were lifted up from the earth, the wheels were lifted up. Whithersoever the spirit was to go, they went, thither was their spirit to go; and the wheels were lifted up over against them: for the spirit of the living creature was in the wheels. When those went, these went; when those stood, these stood; and when those were lifted up from the earth, the wheels were lifted up over against them: for the spirit of the living creature was in the wheels" (Ezek. 1:19–21).

What does this portrayal of the inseparable union of the Spirit of Life with material substance, so many times reiterated, signify, if not that in the manifestation of the universal Life Energy next beyond or within electricity, we contact the very Spirit of Life Itself in connection with this electrical fire of the Lord? The saying has been attributed to Mr. Edison that we might as well spell electricity "G-O-D", and we see how closely he has approached to the truth, for I firmly believe that all this is to teach us that it is a combination of *electrical* and *spiritual* power, functioning through the uplifted sex force of soul complements that is to be the means whereby we shall be liberated from the grosser material of which our bodies are composed, and gradually acquire the more etherial quality of body that can receive from the air the nourishment necessary for its sustenance.

"PUT OFF THY SHOES FROM OFF THY FEET FOR THE PLACE WHEREON THOU STANDEST IS HOLY GROUND."

The question naturally arises that if this be true of one man and woman, why not true of any man and woman joined in legal wedlock? Because, in the first place, this is unquestionably the information intended to be given by the symbol of Aaron's rod budding, and its having the power to remove the murmurings of the children of Israel (the impotence of the capacities or the powers of man, which take rise from his ideas or understanding of the truth—the facts concerning all life) that they *die* not, and the emphasis laid on the fact that the *stranger* that came nigh was to be *put to death*. But independently of this, by this new understanding there is found to be present in the love relation of true spiritual mates, an element of sacredness and worship which I believe you will agree with me is anything but commonly experienced. The chastening that the soul has received before it is able to find its mate, and the rest found in the union with the other soul through the Christ consciousness, produces a *quality of love* that can exist only between two such individuals, and is necessary as the *magnet* to attract the current of electrical and spiritual force, which alone possesses transforming power. In this, as everywhere throughout the universe, the spiritual and physical are related, therefore, the right spiritual conditions are necessary before the right physical conditions can exist.

An interesting example of this interrelation of the elements of the universal substance with spiritual realities, and the constancy of this relation in all modes of expression is brought to our attention in this connection. For instance, we are told that the solar ray corresponding to the planet Mars is red, and its metal, iron; and in this further example we find the color red associated with the metal iron. Red is the color corresponding to the qualities typified by the sign of the Bull (or ox), which in their higher aspects as seen to be strength, and pure ardent love. These qualities, Ezekiel, in calling attention to the ox in his description of the "living creatures" shows us to be necessary to produce the super-man, whose possibilities are seen, through the meaning of the Holy Name, to be evolved from his present limited life only as he attains a right understanding of the sex capacity, the physical power of which is indicated by the different references to lightning, to be electrical, and in this way *iron* is again associated with the color red through the qualities symbolized by this color; for we know that a soft iron core (or something that has been charged with the drawing power of soft iron) for the armature is necessary before electricity can be drawn from the air by the dynamo. The armature might be revolved indefinitely, but if the magnetic core were lacking, no electricity would be gathered. On the other hand, we know that even with a properly magnetized core, if the whole dynamo could be enclosed under a glass case and a perfect vacuum produced, there would be no electricity gathered for the magnet could not contact with the air.

Now that the union of the souls and bodies of true spiritual mates forms the perfectly equipped dynamo is no mere figure of speech. It is an actual fact. But the union of the articular souls and bodies which are partial expressions of the same complete soul is necessary for the right vibratory conditions to exist both physically and spiritually; for *only* the requisite quality of love, and spiritual understanding of this power can produce in the flesh the properly magnetized *iron core* which is necessary to draw through the mind to the body the transforming effects of the Spirit. In this we glimpse the sweep of the ancient wisdom which declares "that man is the Microcosm, that is to say, the reproduction of all the principles which give rise to the manifestation of the universe, or the Macrocosm."

The right spiritual conditions correspond to the access of the dynamo to the air, for until there is no thought or impulse that can serve as a barrier between the man and woman and the conscious presence of God during sexual congress, the right conditions do not exist; because the secret power of the Holy Name abides in the trinity of dualities—God and man; Spirit and matter; masculine and feminine as Two In One, and in the magnet that can attract the electro-living current which has power to transform physical tissue, the spiritual element predominates.

To the woman must be allowed the initiative in recognizing her mate; this is the working of the law, and when her soul has found its rest, surrender is complete; but this can never be until all the longings of her soul for holy things are understood, appreciated and supplemented by the spiritual aspirations and God-like qualities in the soul of the man. But such surrender does not imply the giving up of individuality, but rather the establishment of perfect equilibrium throughout the whole being, because of the fact that each finds his complement (complete-ment) in the other. For this reason there can be the perfect merging of the two lives into one without deterioration to either, but rather added strength and stimulation for united service and continuous development, which is the plan of the Creator, to be worked out in the spiritual evolution of the race.

But for these conditions to be possible, both must possess a hunger and thirst after righteousness, for not till this continual prayer for righteousness, and worship of the Father can ascend unhindered through the absence of dross in the soul of her mate, can a woman's offering be complete and effective unto life; for the offering of the body merely for the satisfying of the flesh, without the presence of the necessary spiritual impulse and aspiration, possesses no evolutionary possibilities.

This furnishes an index to the kind of character the men of the world will have to possess before they can hope to draw to themselves their true mates. There can be no feigning of genuine merit; no half-way purpose entertained. The men as a whole must "right about face" and realize that spirituality is not a thing to be sought alone by women; that spirituality in no wise deprives a man of any virile quality, but causes him to lose only crude perversities, which some apparently think an indication of masculine valor. We cannot expect to receive the blessings of the Spirit if we are ashamed to acknowledge our allegiance to it. This is not because these are withheld as a punishment, but because we ourselves close the channel through which they can come to us.

It is needless to say that these are not the conditions generally existing with reference to physical union. Indeed, for the most part, it has probably not been thought of; nay, more—with many, such sanctity in connection with this matter could doubtless not be understood. It was of those in this material stage of development that Jesus spoke when he said, "Neither cast ye your pearls before swine, lest they trample them under their feet and turn again and rend you." But all are destined to pass beyond this stage in time, for the Father will draw all men unto Himself.

Nor should the attainment of this standard

on the part of both men and women be thought possible only at some distant future time, or by some recluse; not that temporary retirement may not be profitable for us at times, but we are not intended always to live apart from men. The realization of these conditions centers in a most *earnest desire* and *undivided purpose* to live the highest life, and is by no means impossible in this century and year, by men and women engaged in daily occupation for a livelihood; but with the vision—the vision that lifts the thoughts and aims above and beyond material things and the limitations of the physical senses. Not that material things are not necessary and beautiful at their right valuation; they are absolutely necessary in their tangible rigidity in our present state of development. But until we can grasp the sense of the reality, the greater importance, and beauty and satisfaction of the life of the Spirit—the life lived close to God—we are allowing material things to fetter us and rob us of the sweeter harmonies of life, rather than serve our highest good as they are designed to do.

Our greatest difficulty in believing such attainment possible seems to be in actually fearing to face ideal conditions—to get really close to God and be convinced for ourselves what happiness and possibilities are for us if we take God with us into everything, and do not limit "the Holy One of Israel", as did the Israelites of old, which we are told by the author of Hebrews (who it is evident had such a perfect understanding of this whole subject), was the reason why they could not enter into the rest (liberation from toil and privation, and rest unto the soul) prepared for the people of God, "although the works were finished *from the foundation of the world*." And indeed as long as we insist upon measuring the attainment of the future by that of the past, and refuse to believe it *possible* to realize any given ideal, naturally our own refusal to accept it will necessarily keep us from obtaining it.

Someone said to me not long ago—a minister by the way—"What is the use of having ideals if you are ever going to realize them?" (No, I did not misunderstand him. I have quoted him verbatim, I believe.) My thought in this matter is, What is the use of having ideals unless you *intend* to realize them? Why should we be paralyzed with fright because an ideal which we may be willing to accept as possible "sometime" becomes real? I admit the naturalness of the feeling of awe, if not terror, when we realize that God is actually talking with us through our quickened spiritual comprehension, and like Gideon of old, we cry, "Alas, Lord God: for because I have seen an angel of the Lord face to face." But if we really *want* God and do not turn away, then to us as to Gideon comes the reassuring answer, as from a tender protector leading us through strange scenes and experiences with which we are not familiar, "Peace be unto thee; fear not: thou shalt not die."

Thinking of this capacity of sex as a weakness of the flesh alone that must be yielded to ever so moderately is not the right understanding in regard to it. We should make *no* compromise with evil, and what cannot be done with the conscious blessing, and in the conscious presence of God should NEVER be done. This life energy should be reverenced as an evidence of the presence of the power of the Living God in our bodies. We should not be ashamed of it, but control its physical manifestation so perfectly and completely by a right understanding of its spiritual reality, by high thought and high purpose that as far as our physical comfort is concerned, it is negligible; then use this uplifted power, referred to variously throughout the Bible in connection with the "rod", the "sword" and the "Tree of Life" only when blended in harmony with all the qualities and capacities corresponding to the seven colors of the spectrum, to which we find reference in the mention made of the rainbow in the last verse of this first chapter of Ezekiel.

This is the same lesson which is taught by St. John's symbol of the four horsemen, recorded in the 6th chapter of Revelation, which, by the power of the real truth it portrays will outlive any profanation.

"And I saw when the lamb opened one of the seals, and I heard, as it were the noise of thunder, one of the four beasts saying, Come and see.

"And I saw, and behold a white horse: and he that sat on him had a bow; and a crown was given unto him: and he went forth conquering and to conquer.

"And when he had opened the second

seal, I heard the second beast say, Come and see.

"And there went out another horse that was red: and power was given to him that sat thereon to take peace from the earth, and that they should kill one another: and there was given unto him a great sword.

"And when he had opened the third seal, I heard the third beast say, Come and see. And I beheld, and lo a black horse; and he that sat on him had a pair of balances in his hand.

"And I heard a voice in the midst of the four beasts say, A measure of wheat for a penny, and three measures of barley for a penny; and see thou hurt not the oil and the wine.

"And when he had opened the fourth seal, I heard the voice of the fourth beast say, Come and see.

"And I looked and behold a pale horse: and his name that sat on him was Death, and Hell followed with him. And power was given unto them over the fourth part of the earth, to kill with the sword, and with hunger, and with death, and with the beasts of the earth."

The word "beast" in this connection, referring to the beasts which spoke, does not have a bad meaning as one might think. It comes from the Greek word "zoön", meaning "animal" or "a living being", and is rendered in the revised version "living creature " as in Ezekiel. The term "living creature" does not necessarily carry the idea of an animal of the lower order. It could mean a human being or a superhuman being, as *life* or *something alive* is the predominating thought. It is not the word used in the 1st verse of the 13th chapter, which is translated "beast", and which means "wild animal".

This symbol emphasizes the same truth as the vision we have just been considering. The horse typifies passion in its relation to the vitalizing principle in Nature. The first horseman rides a *white* horse. This then represents the *spiritual* reality of passion, blended in the true proportion with other necessary qualities, for all the rays of light blended into one in the ether, which corresponds to the realm of the Spirit, produce white light. Notice that the horseman wears a crown—the symbol of governing power—

and goes forth conquering and to conquer. This is the power that will eventually conquer all evil and limitation (or misconception of the truth, arising from our incompleteness), and bring all into subjection to the Kingdom of the Spirit. The symbol of the bow we shall not desecrate with words. Its sanctity is inviolable.

The second horse is red. This indicates that the qualities typified by the seven solar rays have been separated in the prism of the psychical plane—mind—which is represented throughout the Bible by water (hence the prismatic power suggested in this figure), and the red ray standing alone, not balanced by the others, will necessarily manifest in its lower aspect; Therefore this horseman's weapon could not refer to the sword of the Spirit, but to the weapon of strife gendered by anger and lust, which has power to hurt in every way.

The third horse is black. Some might think this to be an evil indication. Quite to the contrary, it affords the key to the whole truth. Black is the color produced when all the colors are combined in matter. Paints of the seven colors of the spectrum, when mixed, will produce black. The truth taught here is that physical desire—a quality belonging to the red ray—must not be the first nor only cause for physical union, but that a balance of *all* the qualities of character, the corresponding colors of which produce black when combined in material substance, must be brought to bear upon *matter* before any evolutionary effects can be produced.

It is needless to say that the response of the physical organism must necessarily be present in union for change to be effected in the physical body, but not until the body has been crucified and risen again—that is, physical appetite and passion brought thoroughly under the control of the will, and permanently subjugated to the mandates of the aspiring soul, have we gained the mastery over the flesh that is necessary to enable us to receive the gift of a quickened spiritual consciousness, and to comprehend the actuating motive and power by which this physiological change can be brought about.

Thus in the matter of our food, to count eating our greatest pleasure, and burden the stomach with quantities of food not necessary for our nourishment, is gluttony; though there is nothing wrong about enjoying our necessary food. In fact, unless the food is grateful to the palate, the digestive processes are not properly stimulated, but the matter of control is always an essential factor to one's well being and self respect. And thus the right use of the sex function centers about control, associated with an intelligent understanding of its meaning, and with spiritual aspiration. But these matters will naturally adjust themselves through the spiritual growth necessary to lead one to completion.

So we have symbolized by the black horse exactly the same qualities as by the white horse, but the latter refers to the spiritual realities, represented by all the color rays blended into white light, while the former typifies the physical manifestation of the qualities associated with these same color rays converged again in matter (applied to our bodies) after having passed through the psychical prism—the mind—each being rightly understood. And in this connection we note with interest from the 8th verse of the 6th chapter of Zechariah that it was the *white* and *black* horses that went forth into the *north*, which quieted the spirit of the angel, as related in the account of this prophet's vision in regard to this same truth.

The horseman carries a pair of balances. This has no reference to famine or privation, but signifies the exact equilibrium which must exist between the forces of Spirit and matter in this connection. And note the ratio of the spiritual and physical. Wheat refers to the spiritual reality of the fire of the Lord; barley to the physical element. But three measures of barley can be purchased for the price of one measure of wheat; hence the value of the spiritual element is seen to be threefold that of the physical. The caution is given to hurt not the oil and the wine, meaning the light and understanding of the life of the Spirit, three-fourths of the efficacy of this capacity residing in the spiritual actuating motive, and a right understanding of the purpose of the existence of this law. This constitutes its use as "HOLINESS UNTO THE LORD"—the words that were to be graven on a plate of pure gold, and worn by Aaron upon his forehead.

The fourth horse is pale. This signifies passion suppressed unduly or killed. This has been considered the preferable course in regard to this matter by some earnestly desiring spiritual development. It is the natural conclusion (when we have advanced far enough for this matter to disturb us at all) until our eyes are opened to the whole truth. Then we find that desuetude of this function is not the goal to be sought; nor its complete transformation into other channels of creative work: neither is its sole purpose that of procreation. When we are willing to offer upon the altar of sacrifice anything which we *think* stands in the way of our spiritual growth, including this tendency of the flesh, then as in the allegory of Abraham offering up Isaac, lo, a voice calls to us out of heaven, "Lay not thine hand upon the lad", and a proper sacrifice is seen to be provided, which we find involves the offering of every atom of our physical bodies as well as our souls, as a "living sacrifice" upon God's chosen altar, with the result of overcoming hunger and death and hell (Hades, the grave), which followed in the train of the horseman on the pale horse.

It is just this necessity for the exact equilibrium of the understanding between the values of the spiritual and physical elements of this sacrifice that makes the gate so strait and the way so narrow, for while this power must be used and not slain, the physical feature must be understood to exist not as an end in itself, but as a means for the proper working of the law upon the tissues of our bodies. On the other hand, the response of the sensory neurons *must* not be thought of as wrong or impure in *itself*, or the *thought* of guilt will become a barrier between ourselves and God. This normal activity of the sex organs was instituted by the all-wise Father as truly as the normal action of heart or lungs. Without this stimulus in both male and female these organs could not perform their work; hence fertilization would be impossible, and consequently the propogation of the race would be impossible. Then if it is intended by the Creator, why should we attempt to destroy it—that is, its high and rightful use? And why have some most concerned about their spiritual welfare felt they should destroy its natural expression? Because, in the last analysis, they have not yet grasped its highest significance (their experience may not have enabled them to do so), and consequently have not felt it to be in accord with the thought of God. Indeed, the almost universal conception of its use has not been in accord with God's thought, and as long as one sees in this capacity no higher significance than mere gratefulness to the flesh, he may know he has not comprehended the divinely beautiful truth involved. Only through the worship of worth, and the longing to get close to God, with the yearning to help everyone else to want Him and find Him, can one be led to the vantage point where he is enabled to formulate a right conception of this matter. But when we pause to consider the attraction of sex in the light of its origin, its most sacred meaning, and the importance of its office, our pseudo-idealism which causes us to pronounce God's work unholy, is seen to reflect only our grossly inadequate conception of its full meaning, and assumes a humiliating aspect.

It seems reasonable to think that as our bodies become less and less dense, approaching the rarity of the spiritual body, the exchange of the electro-living current necessary for their continued revitalization, through stimulation of circulation and dissemination of creative energy, could take place readily by mere proximity, and that the law as it operates now would give place to this method. But the bridge over which the race *must* pass from *man to super-man*—to be able to overcome physical limitation, death and the grave—is that hunger and thirst after righteousness, and the fulfilling of the Law of Love toward all our fellowmen, which awakens our spiritual senses, till being made perfect in love, we are borne by this circumstance or that, on the tide of that great Law of Life, to which distance is no barrier, back to the one perfect love relation for us, and we can see as with the eyes of God, the purity of all his works, and come to want God with us in every thought and act of life, and thus be able to use the law effectively as it operates in our present state of existence.

That the physiological result is effected by the union of electrical and spiritual power is made clear enough. Just what the nature of the process is cannot be so certainly affirmed, but to me it seems reasonable to think of it simply as a mild and gradual process of electrolysis—disintegration by means of the electrical current—finally leaving us in possession of bodies of the more etherial substance that we are told occupy the interstices of our coarser physical bodies. This power of the electrical current over certain substances we know has been experimented with in the medical world as a means of disintegrating tumors and calculi, but a prominent specialist in electrical therapeutics tells me that it is not practical for this purpose for the reason that if a current sufficiently strong to effect the diseased parts is used, it also breaks down the surrounding healthy tissues. But this effect is just what would be anticipated and required (produced of course by an almost imperceptibly gradual process) to liberate us from the grosser physical matter of our bodies, and cause them to be transformed into the spiritual state without being put off in death.

A summary of the Biblical data as to there being a complement for every person; the reasons given why the measure and quality of love necessary to work the transformation of the body can exist only between two such individuals; the purpose mentioned in the 2nd chapter of Malachi of God's making "one" being that "he might seek a godly seed", etc. but serve to confirm and supplement Darwin's theory of the importance of sexual selection as a factor in the evolution and progress of man. And the late Ernst Haeckel, whom we know would not base a conclusion on anything but the most material evidence, says in "The Evolution of Man":*

"But if we bear in mind how extremely important a part this relation of the two sexes plays in the whole of organic nature, in the life of plants, of animals and of man; how the mutual attraction of the sexes, love, is the mainspring of the most heterogeneous and remarkable processes—in fact, one of the chief mechanical causes of the highest development of life—we cannot too greatly emphasise this tracing of love to its source, the attractive force of two erotic cells. . . . So wonderful is love, and so momentous its influence on the life of the soul, or on the different functions of the medullary tube, that here more than anywhere else the 'supernatural' result seems to mock any attempt at natural explanation. Yet comparative evolution leads us clearly and indubitably to the first source of love—the affinity of two

---

* Vol. II, pp. 695–696.

different erotic cells, the sperm-cell and ovum (erotic chemotropism)."

If Haeckel, honest in his conclusions from tangible evidences alone, could have grasped the fact that the spiritual reality is the first cause of things material, these wonderful results which he could plainly see to be the effects of love would not have mocked "any attempt at natural explanation." Right in this confession he unconsciously admits the inability of physical science, unaided by spiritual understanding, to fathom the meaning of existence and light the way for the continual advancement of mankind.

Does not this attraction between the male and female cells, of which Haeckel speaks, answer to the attraction between the positive and negative elements of electricity? And have we not then in this "erotic chemotropism" of Haeckel; in the modern electromagnetic theory of matter; in the allegorical accounts of the thunder and lightning associated with the Holy Mountain; and in Ezekiel's symbolical reference to electricity as the vehicle of the very Spirit of Life Itself, a series of related evidences sufficient to convince us of the unlimited re-creative, no less than creative possibilities of this fire of the Lord—this physical manifestation of the Christos—when employed with an intelligent understanding of its nature and purpose, and under the right spiritual conditions as "HOLINESS UNTO THE LORD" (LAW), even to the extent of causing our bodies to attain to the spiritual state without passing through death? For if the scientist could trace to "erotic chemotropism"—the beginnings of love—such "supernatural" results in the physical organism, through the medullary tube (the earliest form of the spinal marrow), what may we not look for from the principle of sexual selection carried to its ultimate issue in reunited soul complements, whose love has been chastened and intensified, whose Spirits must have found their home in God ere they could recognize each other; who thus in purity of thought combine the power of the spiritual and physical reality of this Creative Energy, and do not "limit the Holy one of Israel" in power to fulfill his covenant by refusing to believe it possible to be done. And owing to the fact that this power is seen to be available only through spiritual development, is it not easy to see the unity of physical and spiritual science; to read a new meaning in life's experiences, and catch the trend of the whole creation plan?

We find the active principle and motive power of life to be love, and its fruition happiness; this in greater measure as we continually ascend toward the glories that "eye hath not seen, neither ear heard", but the vistas of which will open before us as we make real in our lives the extent of the possibilities just next beyond, which our present light reveals along our path.

We are well aware that it was not Haeckel's thought that there was any spiritual power manifested in the force which he terms "erotic chemotropism"; but rather that the soul itself was but the result of certain phenomena of matter, and ceased to exist at death. However, our interest centers not around his conclusions, but rather his observations as to the facts of the remarkable power of this Creative Force, whose decision as to the importance of such discoveries we know would not rest on any but the most satisfactory evidence from a materialistic point of view, bringing more strongly into the light the solid facts to stand an enduring monument to the real efficacy of the Life Force to accomplish its creative, evolutionary and re-creative work in the world. Thus we see the reference to the Christos, "whose goings forth have been from of old from everlasting", descending into matter to redeem it, and lift up all to a consciousness of God, is not merely a mystical phrase, but does indeed denote the divine reality of a scientific fact; and the scientist who is sufficiently spiritual, or the religionist who is sufficiently unbiased to study the subject in its twofold physical and spiritual aspect, is justified in drawing different conclusions from the same facts than Haeckel has done.

For the sake of those who may yet be inclined to regard the belief that we may live eternally without passing through death as merely a visionary theory or feminine fancy, may I be permitted to refer again on this subject to the thought of Judge Troward, whose opinions are held in esteem by an international following. That he really believed this to be possible is clear from these words:

"Now, evolution is a continuous process of

building-up, and what makes the world of today a different world from that of the ichthyosaurus and the pterodactyl, is the successive building up of more and more complex organisms, culminating at last in the production of Man as an organism, both physically and mentally capable of expressing the life of the Supreme Intelligence by means of Individual Consciousness. Why, then, should not the Power, which is able to carry on the race as a perpetually improving expression of itself, do the same thing *in the individual*? That is the question with which we have to deal; in other words, Why need the individual die? Why should he not go on in a perpetual expansion?

"This question may seem absurd in the light of past experience. Those who believe only in blind forces, answer that death is the law of Nature, and those who believe in the Divine Wisdom, answer that it is the appointment of God. But, strange as it may seem, both these answers are wrong. That death should be the ultimate law of Nature contradicts the principle of continuity as exemplified in the Lifeward tendency of evolution; and that it is the will of God is most emphatically denied by the Bible, for that tells us that he that has the power of death is the Devil (Hebrews 2:14). There is no beating about the bush; not God but the Devil sends death. There is no getting out of the plain words."

Anyone not familiar with that invaluable book—"Bible Mystery and Bible Meaning"—should not fail to acquaint themselves with it. The fact that to the author was not revealed the exact method of this "Lifeward" Law's operation (the reunion of soul complements through spiritual evolution), which brings about the conditions that make it possible for the Law to act upon the substance of the body directly as well as through the mind, and that in consequence, his work sets forth only an exposition of the general principle in its universal application, in no wise confutes the interpretation of the particular application set forth in this volume; but instead, strengthens the evidence of its truth, in view of the fact that his conclusions drawn from study along general lines only, coincide so perfectly, as far as he has carried them, with the underlying truth of the individual application apparent from other lines of approach. His reference to the Devil as being the cause of death is verified in the fact that only by overcoming the Devil in this particular—wrong and impure thoughts in regard to sex—can we lay hold of this power that is provided for the continuous life of the body.

Does any doubtful one still say: "Would you tell us that *this* of *all* things could be the means of the eternal life of our bodies?" Remember that this was God's provision for creating the physical body you now have; and that this manifestation of his Creative Power, when the evidence is in from both sources—material and spiritual—should be seen to be his plan for continually re-creating it, need hardly be surprising. We see this foreshadowed in the sign of the covenant. Why should the phallus be chosen rather than any other organ of the body to bind the covenant between God and man? Does not the time-honored rite of circumcision now seem to point to the correctness of the revelation of the symbology of the Tabernacle?

Moreover, what is really more impracticable about living eternally than about living one day? Life *itself* is the wonder; but we do not stop to consider this because we see it about us continually; but one compelled to speak could no more convincingly contend that we may not live eternally than he could accurately explain just *how* we live at all. Yet we *do* live. Death is the unnatural thing; and we have lived in the delusion that men must always die. But this is only following the natural order of physical, mental and spiritual evolution, for "The last enemy that shall be destroyed is death."

CHAPTER VI

A Glance at Fundamentals

WITH certain individuals a satisfactory standard of living may be sufficient to inspire them to live to their highest, but with others—many, I believe—a satisfactory theory *about* life is quite essential to enable them to find their poise, and thus be ready to live their best lives. I am therefore presenting my understanding of some few fundamental principles, which I hope may be helpful to others.

In connection with the theory of evil and its origin we frequently hear the expression "mortal mind" as though it were something that belonged to us as human beings apart from God, and many of the explanations we hear given of mortal mind and its effects are very confusing to those inclined to weigh the meaning of words.

In the first place, there is no such thing as mortal mind. All the mind in the universe is the mind of God; our mind is just a part of that mind, and this so-called "mortal mind" is only our limited appropriation of the infinite mind of which ours is a part. This limitation is due to our having evolved from lower forms of physical life, and lower stages of mentality, resulting as yet in an incomplete state of development in comparison to what we are destined to become as we approach nearer a realization of our real nature as one with God.

Take for example the mind of an infant in comparison with that of a mature man. It is impossible for the babe to comprehend everything at once. It has to develop its faculties gradually through experience and observation, but there is no blame in connection with this undeveloped state of the baby's mind. It simply has not had sufficient time to develop. Neither is there any blame in connection with our so-called "mortal mind". It is only incomplete, and has yet to unfold powers of spiritual understanding to greater degrees.

This explains the unreality of evil in the absolute sense. Evil is nothing but the misconception of truth in manifestation, and arises from the varying degrees of incompleteness of the perfect being that man is designed to be. Everything done by him—that which is called good or evil—is originally caused by the urge of the Spirit within, seeking for expression through an instrument as yet very imperfect. This statement gives no license to the evil-doer, for as long as he gives expression to this lack of development called evil, he must of necessity reap the reward of this evil. Nor does it argue that wrongdoing should go unrestrained, but that such restraint should look not only to the welfare of others concerned, but to the uplift of the offender as well; and not be established or carried out on the principle that anything is gained in any way through retaliation or vengeance.

It all resolves itself into the fact that creation is not yet complete. God made the world and brought man from lower beginnings to a state of individual consciousness, and a measure of intelligence, and now He is soliciting man's cooperation to appropriate the powers of infinite life which He has put within each soul. He is striving to make us realize his presence within ourselves, and give expression to this divinity now, in this life, not delaying it to an imagined distant heaven.

Referring again to the little child, through infancy and its early years the mother's watchfulness surrounds it very closely, but as it approaches years of maturity, she allows it to depend upon itself; or if she does not, the child's individuality and independence will not be properly developed. It seems to me just the same way with us as God's children. Through all those ages while we were developing an intelligence, God brought us along the way without our knowing much about it, I fancy. But having arrived at a degree of self consciousness, it is as if God said to each of us: "Now it is time for you to put to *use* the power and ability I have given you, that you may develop your own individuality and higher states of consciousness, until you come to the full realization of what you are—an individual personality, yet identical with the Universal God—and the joy that this knowledge will bring. For if you should not develop through use the faculties already given, it would be impossible for you to attain any higher state of consciousness than you now have, and you are still bound by misunderstanding and limitation; your life is not complete and joyous as I planned it for you from the beginning. *But you have a part to do.* You must work *with* Me from this time on, and while you shall find eventually that all power is from Me, yet you will see how we are one, and still you may have an individual personality and consciousness, given you by this method of development, which is the only means that will obtain the desired end. The meaning of it all may at times baffle your understanding and distress you, but keep faith in my good plan for you, and it will be plain in time, and you will be grateful for it all."

So I repeat it is this same urge from within which causes different results—good and so-called evil—in differently organized and developed brains and minds, just as the same white light will appear red, blue or green through differently colored globes. This may seem impossible at first thought, but that is just what it amounts to when we think far enough back. All of what we call the lower emotions arise from, and are, in greater or less measure, excesses of impulses that have had their place in the creation of the human being, in bringing us from the lower forms of life to what we now are, and as we rise in the scale of being and better realize our unity with all life, these same tendencies become transformed, until, for instance, we find the highest outgrowth of the impulse of selfishness causing a man to lay down his life for his friends, because under certain conditions he would *rather* do it than not.

This is why there is no evil in reality. What we look on as evil is evil in a relative sense, and is only the result of an incomplete, growing condition, though we are apt to forget this as we look out over the turmoil and sorrows of earth. Nor would I underrate the fact that evil as we are accustomed to speak of it is a lamentable thing with which to be associated for those who have passed beyond that stage of development in which the urge of the Spirit causes men to do things, which, to those higher in the scale, seem horrible, terrorizing, but this is the only explanation that is consistent with reason throughout, and it certainly clears the atmosphere for me in thinking of this big question.

In regard to our souls and their relation to

God, I can best explain my thought by an illustration. Imagine a glass filled only with air and sunlight. Let the glassful of air and sunlight represent a soul, saying that the air is God within the soul functioning as mind, and the sunlight is God as Spirit. Of course it is really all one and the same Spirit, but manifesting itself in different ways. As the air and sunlight in the glass would be just a part of the air and sunlight in the room, that in the room would represent God in the whole universe. You can readily see then what your soul is. It is just your individual share of God's mind and Spirit to have and use. This covers the definition of soul as being the limit of consciousness, and shows how at the same time you are in God and God is in you. Your life is your conscious share of God's life, and the fact that you have this individual part of God to realize and enjoy carries with it the responsibility of choice, and of giving expression to this divinity which is in you, or which you are. The garden of your own soul is for you personally to tend.

Thus we see we have a real part to take in the perfecting of our lives, and in doing this we have many things to experience which seem very hard when our conception of God's plan is confused. But when from the heights our eyes behold the completed circle of the bright bow of promise, and we grasp the plan in its entirety, we can see whither we are tending and why, and the reward is seen to be more than worth the struggle. Of this we shall be fully convinced when we have reached a certain point by following *faithfully* all the light we have. We gain more light by deeply *desiring* more, knowing that it is to be found within ourselves because God is there, and that we can find it if we *earnestly* seek for it, for "he that seeketh, findeth, and to him that knocketh, it shall be opened."

Salvation must come to mankind through each individual's having a knowledge of his own true nature as a part of God. His failure to realize this, or the idea of separation, gives him the belief in evil as a power or thing of itself, and before man can begin to live a life of unhindered progress, he must realize that *there is no other force in the universe but God*, and before he can enjoy a rich, full life, he must understand that God's will toward him is *always* good; that God *is* Love. Jesus taught us this, but we have too largely disregarded it. We have looked upon God as a being who could be approached only through the merits of the vicarious suffering and death of a mediator. God does not *want* us to think we must go to Him through such a mediator. In fact, we have not found the vital sense of unity with God as long as we feel that we cannot go to Him direct. The only place in which a mediator enters into the great plan of life is where one with greater light gives it to his brother man, as Jesus did, to enable him to recognize for himself his identity with God, thus joining in *consciousness* man and God.

Jesus taught us that we should glorify God, but would you consider it to be glorifying even a human friend to attribute to his character such atrocious qualities as the traditional interpretation of the Bible has attributed to God? The crucifixion has been taken to mean that Jesus was a sacrifice to appease God's wrath, and make an atonement for our sins, to save us from the consequences of the "fall". But what was the "fall"? Simply the process of our receiving physical bodies through which to manifest life. In this sense Jesus' life and teaching does save us from the consequences of the "fall", which consequences were a sense of separateness from God, but no *wrath* on the part of God. As said before, our unfinished state in the evolutionary process has given rise to the idea of this separateness from God, and God's Kingdom cannot come on earth as long as such a lack of understanding of the wisdom and goodness of his plan of creation prevails in the minds of men, and they continue to consider any part of their being—mind or body—as separate from God, or anything that God has made or instituted to be scorned as unholy. It was indeed Jesus' mission to mediate between God and man in this sense. The sacrifice of his body was to teach us with sufficient force that it might never escape the memory of man till the understanding could grasp the fact that God gave all, even his body (matter), that we might enjoy the fullness of conscious life; that our bodies being a part of Himself, are consequently holy, and that we are destined to inherit life eternal without death of the body when we have been made perfect in love, and everything in our lives, our bodies and all their functions have been brought fully into subjection to the Spirit—have been "lifted up" and given back to God, redeemed by the knowledge that all is God; that all that God has made is good and pure in its spiritual conception, and is thus to be transformed by this thought about it. Jesus realized this truth, but knew the world did not; hence his willingness to make the sacrifice. God's nature is to give, not to withhold; He seeks to give to men through men; and so perforce who sees the truth *will give it* though he be *scorned and spat upon*, and persecuted even unto death.

The lower animal creation gives us the clue to the beginnings of our physical manifestation; Jesus lifted up upon the cross portrays the tremendous truth that these physical bodies are a part of God, and all their functions therefore wholly pure; here the two points that determine the line which indicates the progress of mankind from its lowest beginnings to its transcendent destiny. We are told that at the moment Christ's great sacrifice was finished the vail of the Temple was rent in twain from top to bottom (the mystery of the Holy of Holies of the body was made plain for us to comprehend as soon as our understanding, illumined by the Spirit, could grasp the truth), and the earth did quake and the rocks rent, emphasizing the oneness of the universal substance.

When people realize that the Bible is telling them that God and man are One; that the Life Principle in the universe is the same life and power that is in them, they may learn to use this power to better all their conditions of life. The power is there, infinite in the sense that there is a limitless amount to be used as we gradually learn how to use it. This is the part of the evolutionary process depending on us—to learn to use this power rightly and cooperate with it. We cannot be relieved of our part in this matter and still have the joy of individual life and growth.

It is also necessary to get clearly in mind that the *natural* order of things in God's plan is for good and nothing *but* good to come to us, and that the only thing which keeps it from coming is some obstruction in ourselves *originating* in a lack of knowledge of the whole truth about life. When we understand that we were all destined to be happy, and that the Law of Life is always working for our highest *good*, even though it has to work correctively at times, we will attract good by our right understanding and thinking. People have not realized the possibilities of the mind to work them good or ill. It is essential that we understand ourselves, and bear in mind that we are indeed made in the image and likeness of God, with the power of the Infinite at our disposal to work us good when we understand it, or ill (correction) when wrongly used. We must realize that God's plan from the beginning of creation is happiness for *every* soul, and that everything we experience along the way of life is simply coincident with the stage through which we are passing; that trouble and sorrow will pass away from us with the coming of greater light, which enables us to correct the errors in ourselves. But if we hold the mistaken thought that we are helpless, and have nothing to do about it, our errors are not corrected. "And I say unto you, *Ask* and it shall be *given* you; *seek* and ye *shall* find; knock and it *shall* be opened unto you."

A right understanding of God's nature is the crux of the whole matter. When we really believe that God *is* good, we shall expect good from Him, providing we are living in harmony with the laws of good. When we seek the light within ourselves and realize that God *is* the loving and all powerful Father that Jesus taught us He is; when we learn to find Him in the depths of our own souls, to talk with Him, to go to Him for help in *everything* (not failing to do our part when we can see it); when we can explain to Him every situation that troubles us, no matter how insignificant or how great, and if it be beyond our present knowledge or power to control, leave it to Him to make it all come right, and then TRUST and REST in the assurance that God really *is* our friend—that He *wants* to help us, and that his love and power is more than equal to the occasion so that all will be properly taken care of, then we shall have reached a stage from which we can proceed to gain greater light and power without the suffering through which we have passed to get to this point. It is essential to banish from our minds completely the thought that we have to pray to

God to keep evil from coming upon us. The thing that we are living in, walking in and breathing in, and that is *trying* to flow into us and through us is love and good of every description. It is a question of our honoring God with a sufficiently good opinion of Him to believe and trust that He will do the very best things for us that we will *let* Him do.

Anyone might be willing to accept the benefits of the Law without conforming to the conditions under which good is naturally attracted, but we do not draw good in that way; and furthermore, the thing desired would not prove to be good to us as long as the condition in ourselves which obstructs it were not discovered and removed. This is the underlying truth of the belief that God punishes us for our sins. The laws of God (good) do of necessity keep from us the good we seek as long as there is some wrong condition existing in us which keeps the good from flowing through us, but the whole plan is remedial and kind in that it teaches us that there is something in ourselves that will keep us from happiness until it is removed. The Law is unerring in its working. Good *must* flow through us through force of desire (and using the means at our hands, of course) by the law that like attracts like, in just the proportion that all barriers are removed from within us. And by the same accuracy of the working of the law, our good cannot be delayed after we are ready for it. "We can never be free until we have thoroughly learned the lesson that we *cannot* miss our good. . . . No day can come or go without enriching us to the full extent to which we have developed our capacity to receive." The thing for us to give our attention to is making *ourselves* right.

The hindrance within us may be found to be one or more of many things. It may be ill will toward someone—lack of forgiveness. It may be anxiety or grief; it may be nothing that we are accustomed to call sin; it may be merely a great desire to help people when we have not yet found the proper expression for this desire, causing tension and restlessness. Good, in the broad sense, does not mean only what has been, considered moral. God and Nature and Life are big things, and we are invited to open our eyes and study them as such.

The coming of the Kingdom of Heaven on

earth must be through the *spiritually developed individual*, and this condition cannot be brought about, except by man's right understanding of God's nature, and his relation to God, and by his looking *within* for the light and following his individual guidance no matter what persecution it may perchance involve. There is nothing else of so much importance as that one should be true to his highest sense of right no matter what people may think or say. It is not a matter into which praise or blame enters. The important thing to realize is that you have a straight course to pursue—to follow the light of the Spirit within you—and let the consequences take care of themselves. This may require that you stand alone many times, and through seemingly dark days as far as human encouragement is concerned, but you will sooner or later find it to be worth the struggle if you do stand, and what seemed hard will become easy.

Learn to look for the truth *within yourself*; develop your interior powers for perceiving the truth by communing with the Spirit within you. When everyone has learned to do this, the world will be light indeed, for everyone will have found the light within himself and will let it shine. We all owe it to one another to be *ourselves* and contribute whatever light we may get in our individual way (for we are all just a little different from each other), and thus do our part in helping to enlighten all; and no matter how ideal the standard raised aloft in the cause of the immortal truth, not until attention is directed from organization, system, church and creed to the necessity for each one's applying the truth *individually* and *making himself over* by it as the only means of soul growth, shall we be free from a repetition of the history of all movements founded on the teachings of the seers of the past—the light of the prophetic message veiled in priestly ceremony, the vital spark all but extinguished, and the masses blindly groping for the way.

CHAPTER VII

THE WAY OF ATTAINMENT

WHEN a lawyer of the Pharisees asked the Master which was the great commandment in the law, Jesus answered: "Thou shalt love the Lord thy God with all thy *heart,* and with all thy *soul*, and with all thy *mind*. This is the first and great commandment. And the second is like unto it, Thou shalt love thy *neighbor as thyself*. On these two commandments hang all the law and the prophets." And when this is said, all is said, if we would but *lay it to heart*, for "*Love* worketh no *ill* to his neighbor: therefore *love* is the fulfilling of the law." But how earnestly do people generally heed this instruction, with all that loving their neighbor as themselves implies? How thoroughly does *mutual* sympathy, fair dealing and helpfulness on the part of *all* in every walk of life, extend to every fellow-creature regardless of his race or station, be it low or high? Yet it is just this simple, all embracing love and kindness that is required to fulfill the law and develop us. In this we see the justice of this great natural and eternal Law of Life, whether written or unwritten. If its requirements were concerned with station, or even with hard tests of learning, it would not be fair alike to all. But the lowliest can forgive and love, and rank and erudition of themselves will not further us one step along the way.

I would not advocate the practice of lying sleepless in a warm bed at night, tortured by the thought that doubtless many in the world were at the same time suffering from cold and privation, such as I was wont to do before I understood the principle that sympathizing wrongly with people's suffering, does not help them, and only incapacitates us for rendering real service; *nevertheless*, the *measure* of love and sympathy for all our fellowmen that impels to this solicitude for the comfort and welfare of all is absolutely necessary if we would enter upon the Way of Attainment. As long as we are content to seek happiness and comfort for ourselves alone, we are not in the way of finding happiness. God has created every soul for happiness, and there is nothing wrong about wanting it; the desire is wholesome and right, but the Law of Life operates in such a way that we cannot enter the paradise waiting for us until we have been made perfect in love and the simple explanation of this is that universal, altruistic love is actually the means necessary to develop our spiritual senses to such a degree that we can be guided unerringly to the one personal love relation that means completeness for us — rest unto our souls — and which produces a quality of happiness and contentment that enables us to give still more effective help and uplift to the race.

Being made perfect in love implies an expansion of soul great enough to forgive anyone for anything. Does someone say this is impossible? No, it is not impossible. It may be very hard at times, but the measure of the effort required to do this is our own confidential report on just how far we have progressed along the Way. If you do not feel in your heart that you can do this, work with yourself until you can. There is no use to try to build the superstructure of a beautiful life on an imperfect foundation.

First reach a decision with yourself as to what you most *want* to do. Is it your greatest desire to live the highest life and form a beautiful character, or are you more concerned about securing vengeance—so-called "satisfaction"—for every wrong, real or imaginary? If this latter is your present state of mind, you will probably have to suffer in one way or another for awhile yet; that is, until you have decided that to be *right* in every way is the thing most to be desired. If you already aspire to this, but find it difficult under certain conditions to relinquish all feeling of bitterness, then seek a quiet place alone, become perfectly still, close your eyes, let your thoughts retire within where you can get a good perspective of the whole situation, and think quietly. Think of the truths mentioned in the foregoing chapter; think of the greatness of tenderness; the littleness of hate, and see if you do not find your soul big enough even to pity the offender, and to cause you to want to help him find the Way.

Analyze your feelings on each occasion that arises to learn just *how* you feel and *why* you feel so. By doing this you will discover just where your weakness lies, and will know where your efforts for reform must be directed. Then when you have gotten the lesson there is in it for you, cease to think of the incident. Do not be discouraged if it takes hard work. The hard work in this case will be in learning to let go of some feeling of rancor you are tempted to cherish. But continue to try until you feel that you are master of your spirit, and can quickly *let go* of any unprofitable impulse. "He that is slow to anger is better than the mighty; and he that ruleth his spirit than he that taketh a city" (Proverbs 16:32).

To forgive, however, does not mean that we must feel *approval* of the *fault* of the one forgiven. We are not required to lower our standard of right until it can include the misdeeds of those less developed. But while not loving the deed, we should, nevertheless, love the struggling, evolving doer of the deed, remembering the divinity inherent within him, which is the common heritage of each and all, though so often unrecognized and unexpressed. But this is the very condition which calls for kindly service on the part of those who are farther advanced, to help him find his higher self. If, while knowing an act to be wrong, we can take the larger view, and bear in mind the primal cause of the act—the impulse for greater life and happiness (which all alike are seeking), misunderstood and misdirected—and can look beyond the deed, and wish to help the one whose unenlightened condition caused him to so act, then we may know we have truly forgiven.

The Psalmist tells us that the *secret* of the Lord is with them that fear Him, and *He will show them his covenant.* So here we have it; just the same things we have had for two thousand years, but have not used sufficiently to gain the full benefit. Jesus said, "Blessed are they that do hunger and thirst after righteousness, for they shall be filled." The mere knowledge of this statement will not cause us to grow. We must *feel* the hunger and the thirst for lightness, purity and the virtues that we know to be necessary for building a genuine character. But the longing must be for the *qualities themselves*, independent of any reward or punishment in connection with the matter. When one knows within his own heart that he would rather live a wholesome, honest, helpful life even though this might involve no reward, instead of living a deceitful, common, selfish life and receive a reward (if such conditions could be possible), then he is on the Way of Attainment; and there is no use living on in the delusion that any less earnest devotion to the cause of truth and right, for the sake of truth and right itself, will ever enable one to attain this happiness of completion.

And it is not keeping the eyes fixed upon the reward that will bring it, but rather the searching of our hearts, and the *repeated* endeavor (no matter *how* many times we may have failed), to live to our very highest standard of life. For if we think only of the reward, the spiritual development is not being furthered which alone can bring it, and we are day dreaming of the possession of something we cannot have until we have paid the price. When the heart and purpose is right, the price is not hard, because a loving heart and high purpose that impels to kind and worthy deeds, with patience and trust that keeps faith in God's love and in the unerring working of the Law, which will bring us our good as soon as we are fully ready for it, though it seem long deferred, *is* the price. And if our spiritual aspirations are such as they must be in order to give us the necessary development, these are the qualities we shall strive to attain independently of any reward attached. We are justified, however, in thankfully resting in the assurance that high purpose and endeavor does bear the fruit of happiness.

The truth involved in this principle mentioned is, I believe, the chief reason why "the mystery of God" is also veiled in the New Testament; the emphasis put upon the cultivation of the virtues so often mentioned, and the overcoming of our ordinary faults, for this is what must be accomplished first, in a sufficient measure, in any event; and when we honestly strive to follow Jesus' teaching, the "anointing of the Spirit" will teach us the deeper meaning intended for us when the circumstances of our lives call it forth. I do not believe that Jesus even told his disciples all things in plain words, or why did he say in his last talk with them: "I have yet many things to say unto you, but ye cannot bear them now. Howbeit when he, the Spirit of truth, is come, he will guide you into all truth"? (John 16:12–13). And again: "These things have I spoken unto you in *proverbs*: but the time cometh when I shall no more speak unto you in *proverbs*, but I shall show you *plainly* of the Father" (John 16:25). Since this was the last time Jesus talked with his disciples, he must have meant that he (the Christos) would show them plainly of the Father by means of the testimony of the Spirit; and indeed, in John 14:25–26 we read: " These things have I spoken unto you, *being yet present with you*, but the Comforter, which is the Holy Ghost, whom the Father will send in my name, he shall *teach you all things*, and bring all things to your remembrance, whatsoever I have said unto you."

And so we find it everywhere when we are able to receive it, while the form of presentation of the parables affords a lesson to those as yet able to understand only the literal form of statement. In fact, Paul says in effect to the Corinthians that the reason for his not speaking the *hidden wisdom* to them was that they had not yet applied the first principles of spiritual growth. He says, in 1 Cor. 2:4–10, 14, and 3:1–3:

The Way of Attainment

"My speech and my preaching was not with enticing words of man's wisdom, but in demonstration of the Spirit and of power:

"That your faith should not stand in the wisdom of men, but in the power of God.

"Howbeit we speak wisdom among them that are *perfect*: yet not the wisdom of this world, nor of the princes of this world, that come to nought.

"But we speak the *wisdom of God* in a *mystery*, even the *hidden wisdom*, which God ordained *before the world* unto our glory:

"Which none of the princes of this world knew: for had they known it, they would not have crucified the Lord of Glory.

"But as it is written, Eye hath not seen nor ear heard, neither have entered into the heart of man, the things which God hath prepared for them that love him.

"But God hath *revealed* them unto us by his *Spirit*: for the *Spirit searcheth all things*, yea the *deep* things of God.

"But the *natural* man receiveth not the things of the Spirit of God: for they are *foolishness* unto him: neither *can* he know them, because they are *spiritually* discerned.

"And I, brethren, could not speak unto you

as unto *spiritual*, but as unto *carnal*, even as unto *babes in Christ*.

"I have fed you with milk and not with meat: for hitherto ye were not able to *bear* it, neither yet *now* are ye able.

"For ye are yet carnal: for whereas there is among you *envying*, and *strife*, and *divisions*, are ye not *carnal* and walk as men?'

It is a question of the honest effort to make real one's ideals in daily living; the yearning for the consciousness of genuineness in one's self, which is not satisfied with any amount of commendation from others unless one knows within his own soul that he has met himself face to face, has learned wherein his fault or weakness lies, has striven and has overcome.

This, my sisters and brothers of the Roman Catholic faith, is where your church puts an obstacle in your way of attainment, which is well nigh impossible to surmount, for it offers you in the confessional a substitute for this independent, personal struggle. Do not think this is said with the intent to wound. God forbid. But I should not be kind and fair to you if I did not endeavor to awaken you to the fact that faith in anything to alter the effect of a violation of the law of truth and right, beside your own sincere purpose to overcome the cause which exists in yourself, tends to moral and spiritual blindness—the very thing we must strive to overcome if we are going to develop spiritual strength—and the little falsehoods that you seem to regard so lightly, thinking no doubt a confession is all sufficient to overcome their power, will, by the unerring working of this law, deaden your soul to the recognition of truth, leaving you without the consciousness of an inner guide. But the Kingdom of Heaven is within you, dependent on a state of consciousness, whether in this life or the next, and before you can find it, you must be led into it by this inward monitor. So do not kill it; do not quench the Spirit within you; learn to listen for its leading. But whatever may be the purpose, this is not the result obtained by the confessional.

When we fail of our highest standards of living, as we all do many times, we should go *direct to God* with the sincere purpose of receiving strength in the future. But when there is the thought in the mind of the offender, that all can be made right by confession whenever the offense is repeated, can you not see how it turns your confessional into a license for evil doing, and cheats you of the personal effort that is necessary to develop you? For nothing else can take the place of the individual searching of one's self, and the talking alone with God, or waiting with Him in the Silence to develop spiritual strength. We might as well hope to gain physical strength by letting someone else eat our food for us, as to hope to gain spiritual strength while thinking to evade the consequences of our own thoughts and deeds through the merits of any vicarious agency. If there are souls of strength and sterling worth among you, you are such because of your own innate sense of right and wrong unspoiled, as in the case of Luther, whose sense of right could not tolerate the immoral principle of selling privileges in advance for men to commit sins—unspoiled, I say, regardless of, rather than quickened because of the fundamental teaching of your church. For this lively sense of moral rectitude and such a fearless courage are not the product of the principle that underlies the confessional, which benumbs the undeveloped souls of men with the teaching that there can be in existence *any* power, vested in *any man or institution*, that can grant them absolution from the law of justice and eternal right.

And may this further truth be borne in upon the souls of priests and nuns who are worthy in purpose, who in a mistaken idea of the way, have been willing to sacrifice all for the sake of their highest sense of duty, and to gain the highest spiritual good; that God created all men alike for this completed happiness, and instead of being gained, the highest good is lost by continuing to go counter to God's plan.

Perhaps someone feels that his particular lot is just a little too hard to make possible any progress while in it. I wish I might impress upon each one the truth that the circumstances in which we find ourselves are just what our particular stage of development calls for. There is some benefit to be derived from it; some aspect of the great Eternal Truth to be made plain to us; some quality to be developed; some life lesson in it for us that must be mastered before we are through with it. I mean by this that we have at some time drawn this circumstance to us, or may be even now drawing it to us on account of some incompleteness in ourselves, resulting in the inability to handle such a situation patiently and masterfully. It seems as though the inmost purpose of our souls, which lies so deep that we do not always recognize its presence, is demanding a chance to meet and gain a conscious victory over some weakness for which this or that particular circumstance affords just the proper field of endeavor. When we once realize this, and are convinced that the way to remove the undesirable condition is to examine ourselves and see wherein we manifest imperfections of character, and inefficiency in dealing with the situation, then we are working along the right lines to free ourselves from it. But as long as we hold the thought that we are helpless to change circumstances, and allow ourselves to drift instead of standing at the helm; or as long as we *fret* at any circumstance, and do not give our time to developing the power to meet it patiently, and to overcome our faults which it brings into evidence, we are only wasting our time and putting farther away the day when it will leave us, not to return in the same form or in some other guise with the thumbed page of the old lesson turned up for our perusal.

This should in no wise be taken to mean that because an adverse circumstance has good in it for us that we should accept it as a final lot, thinking that if it is good for us we should not try to change it. Get the point that the only good adversity has in it, after it has broadened our sympathies for all classes and conditions of men, and given us a lesson in values and proportions, is the opportunity for developing the power *to work ourselves out of it*, thereby increasing our total of merit and efficiency; and when a failing has been overcome, we will no longer attract the adverse circumstance coincident to it. Have an ideal; work toward it constantly; never lose sight of it except as it may be replaced by a higher ideal, but be *patient* in overcoming the difficulties that arise in your path of attainment.

But by patience I do not mean a passive attitude that encourages people to impose upon us, which is quite as unjust to them as to ourselves; but rather what we might think of as the resultant of equal parts of forgiveness, courage and hope. Courage is not averse to gentleness. Indeed, it must accompany all endeavor if we expect to bring to pass things worth while. This lack of practical courage to take the necessary action is as likely to be the failing as anything else that keeps one in some undesirable circumstance. This is why many apparently kind hearted, well meaning people are oppressed by this or that condition. One's difficulty may be nothing that is ordinarily looked upon as a fault of character. Nevertheless, Nature has in mind for you the pattern of a complete, well rounded being, and your incapacity in any line will attract an opportunity for you to make that good. This should not be looked upon in the light of a punishment. That is not the idea. It is rather an opportunity brought right to your door to attend the great school of experience without a tuition fee. Here again we see the kindness of the Law, for I believe there is nothing else which will develop you quite as thoroughly and effectively as just the patient, cheerful meeting of the daily trials in the home, office, school-room, factory, or wherever your occupation calls you, looking upon every annoyance as an opportunity for the perfecting of your character; never so much engrossed in your own trials as to forget to sympathize with others. We are not all in a position to give such service as we should like to give, but anyone can serve with a kindly word and smile—the cup of cold water—to cheer another on his way, and this is truly acceptable service.

In the training of children, if the teacher or mother will take a philosophical view of the matter, it will be much easier to be patient. Stop to think what it is that causes the child to act thus or so. What is it that causes one child to strike another if perhaps its toy has been appropriated? or one lad to pommel another if there has been foul play? It is the child's sense of justice finding expression without its being modified by the qualities of tolerance and forgiveness. But time and experience are required to mature these loftier qualities in the child. When we take this more comprehensive view, it is easier to be patient while we explain to all the young offenders the principle of ethics involved. Their wishes have been interfered with and they have made a demonstration of temper.

How much better are we doing if, because our wishes have been interfered with by their acts, we also make a demonstration of temper? Someone may say, "But mine was a just provocation."The child also thinks his a just provocation, and this excusing of ourselves in our own sight instead of striving to bring ourselves up to the standard of holding a right spirit under all circumstances, regardless of what anyone else may be doing, is just what will cause us *not* to grow.

But suppose there may be someone who cannot honestly say within his heart that he feels this deep concern for the welfare of others, which I have mentioned—someone who does not feel the drawing of a high ideal of character building and attainment. Wherein lies help for such? Must he despair utterly? By no means, for God is in *every* soul He has created, only some have not yet become acquainted with their own souls and with God within. When they do, they too will feel this same love, this same aspiration, this same hunger and thirst after righteousness, for which there is *no* substitute.

How then, and where can such a one begin? We always have to *begin* just where we are;

we can omit no step, but the thing to *do* is always to *follow out your highest impulses*. Good impulses allowed to die may be tardy in reviving: good impulses *fulfilled* put you farther on the Way with every hour. Even such impulses as the first feeble urge felt by primitive man to keep himself clean, fulfilled, is uplifting, and lays the foundation for a higher impulse to be felt. Such motives as this we are accustomed to think of as being only material; nevertheless, it is the urge of the Spirit working through an instrument as yet not sufficiently perfected to register a higher impulse, and because of this Spirit within, one good impulse along *any* line, when fulfilled, will leave place for a higher to follow, and thus the Father draws us to Himself.

None are left helpless, no matter from what point they have to start. Everyone has sufficient promptings toward the right to lead him eventually straight up to the full light if he would follow them; if in the battle with himself between right and wrong, he would always *choose* to follow the higher impulse. Here is the starting point in the matter of character building. The individual *must choose* his course. If he is to advance, he must first aspire, and then decide to follow the path along which his aspiration leads, and all his decisions must be made with this in mind. The responsibility of choice is an accompaniment of his individual personality, and the pivotal point in the matter of the attainment of character is the realization that progress in the right direction begins with the *individual choice* of a right ideal, independent of the standards or motives of any or everyone else. Whether he will sacrifice his wrong impulses to his attainment of happiness, perfection and peace, or whether he will yield to them to his continual misery and blindness, his own choice determines. When he reaches an agreement with *himself*, and deliberately chooses to *let go* of any purpose of retaliation, no matter what an offense against him may have been, the tide of the battle has turned in his favor, and he has conquered his arch enemy.

Many lives seem to be a record of intermittent effort in the right direction, and wavering from the true course of progress apparently because they are not sure that it always "pays" to follow ideal standards of living; but if all would adopt the standard of right for the sake of right itself, regardless of whether immediate results seemed pleasant or unpleasant, and heed the promptings that urge them onward and upward, which promptings are in *every* soul, they would not be alternately gaining and losing ground, resulting in such a slow and meagre progress. This it is to seek first the kingdom of God and his righteousness; in other words, to hold your friendship with God, and simple lightness in all ways as uppermost in your life, letting all your affairs adjust themselves in accordance with this standard, and not allowing any other interest—financial or otherwise—to hold the uppermost place and determine how much of lightness you can *afford* to employ in your living.

It seems we must make real in actual daily life each successive step of our ideal of character building, before we can get more light from within ourselves. If we listen to the urge of the Spirit within us, and always follow the highest light we have, we *must* ascend continually; so do not sleep, do not stagnate.

A high impulse may at times find through you but very imperfect or incomplete expression, and perchance being misunderstood, be met with rebuff on the part of someone, tending to intimidate you from again giving expression to the highest promptings within your soul; but do not be disheartened by such a result when you know your motive to be right, for every sincere effort to follow the urge of the Spirit constitutes a right act for you in the sight of the Father, no matter how misjudged by others. And remember the cause of most hurts lies no deeper than misunderstanding, and when this is done away, the universe will be seen to be one at heart.

And do not make the mistake of suppressing the impulse of gladness and mirth, thinking it will hinder your spiritual development. Some appear to think that if they were to live close to God, they would of necessity be sad, denying themselves every pleasure they naturally feel inclined to enjoy. But this is very wrong. We are cautioned against this very thing in Malachi 2:13: "And this have ye done again, covering the altar of the Lord with tears, with weeping and with crying out, insomuch that he regardeth not the offering any more, or receiveth it with good will at your hand."

You are a part of God, and sometimes you

want to laugh. Well, that is God wanting to express mirth through you. If God did not want to laugh, you would not want to, for God is all. God makes you want to sing and dance sometimes, too. To move the body—rhythmically to music is a holy pleasure, provided it is done wholly unto God; that is, if you realize that God gives you the impulse to want to dance, and simply thank Him for the pleasure of it. We are told repeatedly in the Bible to rejoice, in the Lord, and are exhorted specifically to praise Him in the dance; and in Phil. 4:4 we read: "Rejoice in the Lord alway: and *again* I say *Rejoice*." So do not think that being spiritual necessitates being sad. Sadness is injurious to health; it is sinful. We are all sometimes sinful in this way, but we should strive to overcome this as much as any other fault, and should not associate sombre thoughts with worthy qualities, Life lived close to God is the happiest, most cheerful life that we can live. Of course there are states of mind higher, and more sacred and more *enjoyable* than those impelling to laughter, but that is no reason why we should suppress an impulse to laugh if we feel it.

The honest thinker will say at once that if God makes us want to laugh, then we will have to say that God makes us become angry too, and in a way he does; but think just what I said in regard to that before. I said that the urge of the Spirit is the original cause of everyone's doing what he does. But this urge has yet in many cases to come through minds but slightly developed—an incomplete understanding of things. It is not the ultimate purpose of the Spirit to make you become angry, but It has to *let* you become angry temporarily, while you are getting experience which will enable you to better comprehend all phases of the truth, because anger may be the only form of expression you have yet learned to give to an impulse which in itself is high, as in the example given of a sense of justice without tolerance. For let us get clearly in mind that creation is not yet completed; it is continually going on, and when the understanding is more highly developed, the same urge will not cause the same result. When we understand how we are all just in the process of making, it is an easier matter to forgive if someone does what at one time might have greatly offended us.

But when we stop to think that the reason people do wrong is that their understanding is not yet sufficiently enlightened to cause them to do otherwise, the impulse we feel toward them is not just to censure, but to help.

To broaden your horizon and gain a more comprehensive outlook on life, get acquainted with the literature of the New Thought, if you are not already familiar with it. This new philosophy of life, or Truth, as it is sometimes called, affords an uplift that will change despondency to hope. But in saying this it is also necessary to mention the fact that there is much that may be found in book stores under this general caption which must be discriminated against as really harmful. "Prove all things; hold fast that which is good." And among the diversity of opinions, beware of the error that the whole of life can be worked out on any two of the three planes of our existence—physical, mental and spiritual. The writers who, while no less spiritual, are also rational, and recognize the divine and eternal purpose of our triune nature, will be found most helpful to read after; for a conception of the truth no less broad than this is what must eventually bring order out of the confusion that seems to exist in the minds of many authors, and teachers of the Truth.

I have heard it said that one's intellect was a hindrance to his understanding of the Truth! Of course the teacher who said this was anxious to help those seeking light, but did not in this case make a correct statement, and such mis-statements are likely to be very confusing and discouraging to some. The failure to realize the value and importance of spiritual perception is a hindrance to your advancement in the Truth, for this *transcends* mere intellect, but even spiritual perception could not function independently of intellect. The two together might be likened in a way to the powerful telescope in the observatory—the intellect the bulky machinery that holds the lens in place, and spiritual perception the lens itself—but it is evident that either one without the other would not be a perfect instrument. Our intellect is of God just as much as any other part of us, and was given to us to use. The point is to use it to the highest purpose, and *develop* spiritual perception by going at times into the Silence, quieting the physical senses as far as possible, and letting the mind retire to the stillness within. Then *listen* to be taught of the Spirit concerning the truth of life, and carry this knowledge back to the outer consciousness, until more and more the whole mind becomes illumined by the light within. Thus grows the sum of our knowledge of the Truth—the Truth which transforms men—the Truth (facts) which we shall know that will make us free.

And do not fail to study the Bible for its deeper meaning. Your eyes will surely be opened, and you will realize as never before how plainly God is speaking to his children through this *wonderful* Book. This is where my beloved fellows of the liberal faith have thus far fallen short. In their interpretation of the Bible they have done nobly in defending the name of God from infamy, and one would think that glorious Credo a compendium of Holy Writ, but they have missed the *pulse of life* that makes alive those pages, in having failed to *listen* for the heart that throbs beneath the symbols.

If people would but realize that what Jesus taught us is the way to transform *this* life, making *it* continuous and eternal, they would get the full benefit of his teachings; and all the years of man's life after he has reached a certain age would not be wasted, and effort for continued growth, attainment and service paralyzed by the thought of approaching old age and death, instead of the gradual transformation towards the spiritual body and the paradise awaiting him, which he should willingly forego until his services to those of earth who are following on, and earth's service to him is complete.

No one who has faith in the glories of the heavenly life would wish to linger indefinitely on earth in age and decrepitude. Far better lay down the worn out instrument and be rid of it under such conditions. Indeed a little short-sighted selfishness might cause us to want to depart in early life to that fair home, leaving behind the toil and stress of earth. But we all have lessons that must be mastered *on this earth plane*, and we may as well continue to apply ourselves to the work now until we have finished it. More than this, the world needs to be made over. People on earth need all the help that can come to them from those who have grown wise, and capable of giving saving help; and the ability to retain youth and vigor while knowledge and experience valuable to mankind are accumulated year after year by benefactors of the race, instead of such pursuits and services being cut short by death, can readily be seen. This, far more than the beautiful thought of the continuity of life, is the real value of this knowledge.

Eternal life and abundant happiness and prosperity are promised as the blessings of the covenant, to which Jesus tells us we shall attain by keeping his saying. In other words, keeping Jesus' saying—earnestly trying to *practice* his teachings, not just *knowing* them—will cause us to be able to obtain the blessings of the covenant through the only way which insures them in full measure; that is, the possession of the spiritual power to recognize the soul of which one's soul is a part.

Until men realize that their bodies and all their bodily functions are holy, and to be used as "HOLINESS UNTO THE LORD" (LAW), they will continue to lay down the physical body after a certain number of years, and if they have not worked out all of life's lessons sufficiently well to satisfy the Spirit within them, they will reincarnate and come back to earth to work out their experience in matter until they have conquered it— brought it into subjection to the Spirit. But as the spiritual senses of individuals become sufficiently developed for them to be reunited with their soul complements, their bodies may live in continual youth, becoming lighter and less burdensome, eventually drawing nourishment from the air, and warmed by their own electrical vitality, as they are gradually released from heavy physical material and approach nearer to the spiritual body, the vibratory rate of which makes its more etherial substance invisible to the physical eye. But the development of the spiritual powers through altruistic love *must* come first, simply because it is only by means of them that we can obtain this blessing. This is wherein God is the Lord (Good is the Law). God tells us that every knee shall bow, and every tongue confess, and with this new understanding of the truth, it is as if He had added the final Q.E.D. to the proposition which He has been demonstrating through all time.

Ere this the thought has doubtless been in the minds of many of my sisters: "What assurance can I have that my mate is living in the world today?" This, however, is a question that no one can answer definitely for you, and there is no way for you to answer it until you may be drawn to that mate and the right spiritual conditions give rise to the necessary knowledge. Then you will know, and will know that you know. Your mate may not be living. He may have passed on before you; but even if for this cause, or any cause whatsoever, the happiness of perfect companionship be deferred to the spiritual state of existence, is it not a great deal to know that it awaits you somewhere in your ascending career when all conditions are right? On the other hand, there is no more reason to think that one's mate is not living than that he is. The probabilities are that most of the people alive today could be truly mated if they were sufficiently developed spiritually to recognize each other; but this great problem can only be worked out by individual devotion to duty and high ideals. To be *right* in all ways should be our first concern, and only through our efforts to this end are we lifted above the physical and mental, to the spiritual heights where the Law works unobstructed and adjusts this relation as originally planned, whether it be for us in this life or after we have passed out of this body.

When all conditions are right there will be evidence which will convince you beyond any doubt, for it will be more conclusive than the customary feeling of fondness for another which is usually accepted as sufficient ground for marriage. Never proceed on the supposition that someone is your mate until *all doubt* has been removed by this proof. With it will come "rest unto your soul"—its tireless quest rewarded—and you would be willing on the strength of this assurance to pass cheerfully this way alone, if for any cause this might be necessary, rather than be united with any other.

Beyond this I may not tell you. If I did it would fail to be a sign unto you. Or, to state it differently, it would disqualify you for recognizing this evidence from the Spirit. Further, things of such inviolably sacred nature may not be bandied about in print. This, when it comes, will reveal to you what I mean by the soul of the Name.

Do not be tempted foolishly to seek advice from fortune-tellers or mind-readers, or even friends; for this assurance you may have that when all conditions are right, every lingering doubt will be removed through your own interior powers, and depending on any source of information except your own awakened spiritual senses, will only delay your development. No power *outside of yourself* can give you correct information in regard to this matter. It will come to you directly from the Spirit if the one in question is your mate, and you walk close enough to God to understand his thought.

So do not seek a proof, for it will come all *unsought* under the right conditions. Relieve your mind of it entirely; be grateful that God has made you for such happiness, and go about your living with the definite assurance that it is worth while to be your *highest* self under *every* circumstance. And be cheered by the thought that every battle fought and won in your own soul has helped some other one, perhaps tired and disheartened, also to win; for thus is all the world knitted together by the penetrating, radiating power of thought.

There should be men whose hearts are pure enough and courage strong enough to unify and teach this truth, with precept emphasizing the necessity for scrupulous personal examination, and self reliance in the matter of spiritual advancement, for this is the gospel that must be preached in all the world to every creature. But let any such beware lest they make known the finished mystery without emphatic warning to all men; for should the mass of men who might be incapable of appreciating the spiritual purport of this message—whose stage of development enables them to understand only the physical element of this function— think that because the sex power is thus approved of God, that it means less of self control instead of more, and abandon themselves to the thought of the physical, even in one instance of cohabitation, they would, because of the capacity of the masculine body, surely bring upon themselves the torments spoken of in Revelation IX, which stands as a warning for safe-guard against the revealing of this truth of which I speak. The language is figurative, but the physical torment (through the power of thought to effect chemical change in physical tissue) would be real.

Do not think Revelation to be merely an altered Jewish apocalypse, but hear the word as written: "I Jesus have sent mine angel to testify unto you these things in the churches (avenues of approach to God, whether individual or universal). I am the root and the offspring of David, and the bright and morning star." Revelation is a disclosing of the divine mysteries, and a prophecy written after Jesus' time—a storehouse of information which only the "key of the house of David" will unlock. It is a masterpiece of symbolism, some of its most terrorizing imagery being simply statements of inspiring truths. However, the reference to the 9th chapter should be heeded as I have cautioned you. I beg each man *individually* not to think this merely *speculation*, nor that I am surely cautioning some one else. I mean *every* man. I HAVE WARNED YOU. And let each reader make it his personal care to communicate no disconnected part of this information to anyone without the accompanying warning I have given.

The curtain thus drawn aside, affords a long look ahead. We see God's plan for the continuity of life, and a paradise of happiness eventually for *every* soul; we see the hopes and aspirations of youth, and the desire for the cultivation of our God-given faculties not abandoned in discouragement if unfulfilled in early years, but enriched and ennobled by experience and increasing knowledge of the Truth, and inspired by the thought of opportunity for continuous development along all lines, being realized in greater measure with the added years. For we find the road leads not to the crest of the hill for half the way, and then down on the other side, but is an ever ascending path that grows brighter and brighter unto the perfect day, when "The kingdoms of this world are become the kingdoms of our Lord, and of his Christ."

It is of perfected earthly conditions that the vision is related in Revelation XXI, when this *tabernacle of God* will be with men. Notice it is to be with *men*, not referring to a state of existence with which we are not familiar, and the promise is that there shall be no more death. The promises have been preserved for us, secure against attack, through our long night of misunderstanding; let us now go forth into the glad morning of the new day just dawning, cheered and refreshed by the reasonableness of the hope for conditions of life and happiness on this earth that have hitherto been thought too ideal to be made real.

"And I heard a great voice out of heaven saying, Behold, the tabernacle of God is with men, and he will dwell with them, and they shall be his people, and God himself shall be with them and be their God. And God shall wipe away all tears from their eyes; and there shall be no more death, neither sorrow nor crying, neither shall there be any more pain: for the former things are passed away."

THE END.

www.ingramcontent.com/pod-product-compliance
Lightning Source LLC
Chambersburg PA
CBHW071501040426
42444CB00008B/1441